AF269060

Casual Observations

David Hinkle Southard

Copyright © 2021 by David Hinkle Southard.

Library of Congress Control Number: 2021900964

HARDBACK: 978-1-954673-26-7
PAPERBACK: 978-1-954673-25-0
EBOOK: 978-1-954673-27-4

All rights reserved. No part of this publication may be reproduced, distributed, or transmitted in any form or by any electronic or mechanical means, without the prior written permission of the publisher, except in the case of brief quotations embodied in critical reviews and certain other noncommercial uses permitted by copyright law.

Ordering Information:

For orders and inquiries, please contact:
1-888-404-1388
www.goldtouchpress.com
book.orders@goldtouchpress.com

Printed in the United States of America

Contents

1 Research

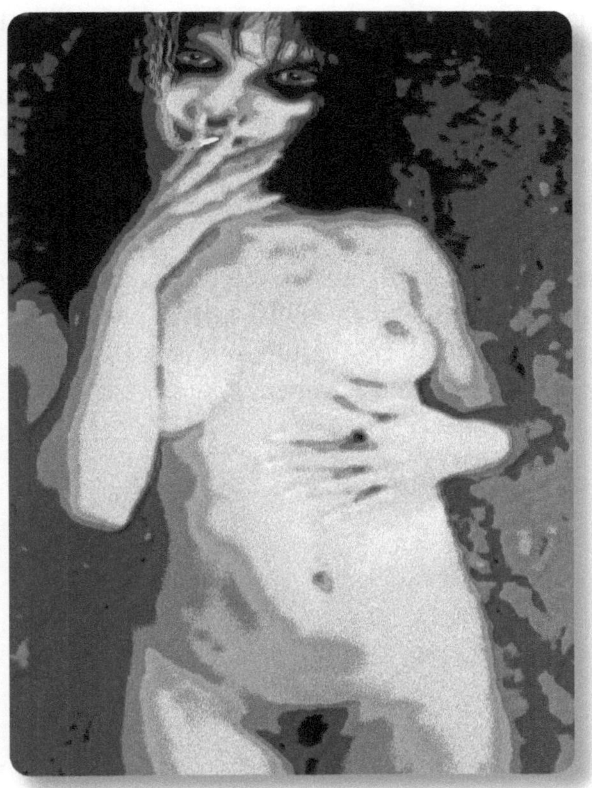

"What are you looking at?" She bent down and looked over his shoulder.

"Well...I want to write erotic stories that have realistic characters, plots, and climaxes, no pun intended." He laughed.

"Mmmmmm. Sounds like you'd rather write about sex than have sex," she said.

"Possibly"—he shook his head—"but I hope not. Lately, I've been studying all the different ways we've dreamed up to have sex—all our perversions. Mostly I do my research on porn sites. I am studying several hours a day."

"Studying? I can see that. Mostly on porn sites, just for research, you say?"

"Yeah. Just to get a clearer idea..."

"You and a million other old perverts...I mean, old men." She bent her face closer to his laptop's screen. "What the hell is she doing? Is that normal?"

"I'm not sure. Listen, I'm only looking at porn to excite my imagination in order to paint illustrations for my stories."

"Jesus! I didn't know that was even possible," she said, and straightened up. "How did she get into that position?"

"That's a good question. You can see I have a lot to learn—that I'm researching diligently. After I become an expert, I'll share all my knowledge with my beautiful wife. You can test me out and see if I learned any valuable lessons."

"*Estás delirante.*" She laughed. "You're delirious."

2 To the Flame

Surprised by the aged face
Reflected in the bright, hot,
Streaked window glowing
Black, cleaned, and rinsed
By tropical storms past.

In the mirrored image
An unambiguous message,
All vulnerability swept away,
A life written between the lines
Of the wins and losses
Experienced and forgotten
And painted on the dark glass.

Acknowledged in an instant,
The clear reeling premonition
And undeniable validity
Of destiny's demand to return
And surrender to the intoxicating
Passion found on a new continent.

Suddenly filled with desire,
Motivated to haste through
Impatient anticipation.
The long for return decided,
Charged with certainty of
Prophesized ecstasy and
Soaring self-immolation.

—Miami, 2013

3 Vegetable Soup

A beam of light from the full moon entered the open door of the back porch. Slid across the polished linoleum and moved down the hall. The moon's silver light silhouetted her body through the thin white material of her robe. Magnolia-scented air filtered through the gauzy curtains that framed the window. The garden patio three floors below bathed in platinum.

She pulled her hair back and tied the long, thick strands together behind her head with a black silk ribbon.

"Women are just genitals in the eyes of men," she said.

She carried a saucepan over to the small white gas range, picked up butane lighter, and lit a front burner and turned the flame up high. She used a wooden spoon to stir the soup left over from lunch to keep it from burning. Her free hand pulled and held her robe together as her hips moved unconsciously to the rhythm of the spoon making a figure eight through the thick vegetable soup.

"Tits and asses are all we are to you." She adjusted the flame under the saucepan until the ring of blue-tipped flame all but disappeared. "Sex objects—pussies are all we are to you. Makes me tired thinking about it."

She made a chopping sign with the hand that had held the robe closed to make her point. A breast with an erect brown nipple pushed out. With no conscious effort, she drew the sliver of the robe's thin material back and covered the nipple. Two long lines formed by the open front of the white robe against her dark skin fell down the curve of her belly and past her pubic hair, kissed the insides of her long, muscular thighs, slid past her calves but gave out before landing on the pedicured red nails of long, slender brown toes.

"All you men see women as vaginas, I swear."

She opened the varnished door of the cabinet above the counter, picked out two white porcelain bowls, handed them down on the tiled surface of the counter. She picked up the saucepan and ladled out equal amounts of soup into the bowls.

"Soup's on," she said. "Set the table and I'll bring the bowls of soup. Grab the new loaf of French bread from Carrillo's Bakery—the kind you like—baked in a steam oven."

She carried the bowls to the dining room table and set each on a place mat her best friend had given her as a gift from Peru, sat down at the end of the table, and crossed one leg over the other. The bottom edges of the open robe fell to the floor past the legs of her chair, exposing a long, slender leg.

"Soup's left over from lunch. My housekeeper prepared it with potatoes, celery, *champiñones*, broccoli, cauliflower, carrots, and chicken stock. She used Daddy Hinkle's Original seasoning to flavor it. Pass the bread, please."

She broke off a large chunk of the french bread and dunked it into the soup. She took a bite of the soaked bread and a drop of soup ran down the edge of her wide mouth.

"What are you waiting for? Eat your soup."

4 You Don't Own Me

"My pussy belongs to me," she told him.

"Okay," he said.

"*Soy una feminista.*"

"Good. I like feminist and independent women who think."

"My father told me that a woman's pussy was hers to do with what she pleased."

"Good," he said. "Your father was right."

"I heard him say it when I was four years old," she said. "No man can dominate me."

"I don´t want to dominate you."

"You never will; my pussy belongs to me."

"I don't want to own you," he said.

"Fucking me is all you ever think about," she said.

"Yes, all the time." He laughed. "You're too sexy and you know it."

"My first husband was too big," she said, "and he didn´t taste good. I didn´t like the way he smelled."

"You like the way I smell?" he said.

"I like the way you taste, too," she said.

"I am not very big," he said.

"No," she said, "but I love the way you fuck me."

"Your pussy is very exotic," he said, "and very delicious."

"My pussy belongs to me," she said. "I can do with it what I want."

"Good. Do you want to fuck me?" he said.

"Yes," she said. "Yes, I do."

"Fucking me is all you ever think about," she said.

"Yes, but not all the time," he said. "Sometimes I am distracted by other things."

"Not when you´re around me, you´re not," she said. "My first husband left me alone at home and went out drinking with his friends. He would bring them over. They would all be drunk. He expected me to cook for them and serve them."

"He was a fool, your husband."

"I told my philosophy professor that I wouldn´t serve drunk friends of my husband. He told me that I should. Because to serve her husband is a wife´s duty, my professor told me. He was like all the rest," she said.

"I will cook for you," he said. "I want to serve you, too."

"You already do," she said.

"Because I´m an American." He laughed. "We live to cook and clean up after our women."

"What you live for is to fuck me," she said. "I clean up after myself."

"That makes two of us," he said.

"You are lucky to have me," she said. "You are lucky I agreed to marry you, a *gringo*. I can't believe I married *un americano*."

"Yes, I´m the luckiest *americano* in the world. I like cooking for you, but I really like washing the dishes after lunch." He laughed.

"What you like is my hot pussy," she said.

"Yes, even though your pussy doesn´t belong to me."

"Nor to any other man," she said. "My daddy told me my *cuca* was mine."

"I love your *cuca*."

"My first husband thought he owned me. He tried to dominate me," she said. "I knew I would divorce him even before I married him, but I wanted to get to a big city—to escape to Bogotá."

"You escaped all right."

"I hated the way he acted. He was too big," she said, "but he was my ticket out of the jungle. He was pure *costeño*. He came from a rich family and was eight years older than me."

"I'm almost twenty years older than you," he pointed out.

"You´re not old," she said. "Help me off with these boots."

"Now my jeans, but not the socks," she said. "It´s too cold."

"You have beautiful legs. I love the color of your skin." He pulled her pants down.

"One time, the *Costeño* beat me for not having his lunch ready. He locked me in the bedroom so I couldn´t get away. I put fourteen stitches over his right eye with an ashtray," she said. "No one can dominate me!"

"Even me?" he said.

"Especially not you. Do you like my panties? You remember when we bought them?" she said. "Do you remember where?"

"Yes, I remember. I like the bra too," he said. "Mostly, I like your beautiful legs."

"We bought them in that little town outside of Barcelona, remember? You made me cry because I made reservations to fly to Granada, and we had to take a train to that little town and catch the flight there instead of out of Barcelona."

"It broke my heart to see you cry," he said. "I didn´t care about the reservations."

"You like the color of my panties? The color of violets," she said. "You bought me the most expensive ones."

"I like the color of your *cuca*," he said.

"You like to watch me when I touch myself is what you like," she said. "All you think about is sex."

"Yes," he said, "how could I not when I´m with you?"

"You like the *café con leche* color of my skin and my hot, dark *cuca costeña* is what you like."

"Yes," he said. "I love the chocolate color."

"You only think about *follandome* all the time. It's what you think about all the time. Pull my panties off me. Pull them off! You like to see me touching myself, don´t you?"

"You are too beautiful." He pulled her panties off and threw them on the floor.

"I´m so excited. I want to see you too. Let me see you! You´re not so small. I want to feel you inside of me."

"Yes!"

"Follame."

"My cuca is yours."

"It belongs to you, *sólo a ti*."

"Only you!"

5 Hot Chocolate

She reached around behind her to a shelf on the wall opposite the stove. The narrow shelf matched the tight galley kitchen of the otherwise spacious third-floor apartment. She picked a wooden spoon out of a terracotta pot full of kitchen utensils: spatulas, a potato masher, a vegetable peeler with a rubber handle, large stainless-steel spoons, and a long wooden scraper. She laid the spoon across the top of the saucepan on the stove top and opened the door to the cabinet above and to the left of the gas range.

The bottom of her blouse rose up over the waist of her jeans and revealed the small gold pin piercing her belly button as she stood on her tiptoes to reach into the top shelf. She did not have to use the stool the housekeeper always used to pull down a package of *panela* she found at the edge of the shelf.

Her small breasts pressed against the silk of the blouse as she levered back up on one slender foot to reach the box of dark unsweetened chocolate in the back of the same shelf.

She opened the box of chocolate, broke off three large pieces, tossed them into the saucepan, added half a cup of panela, a stick of cinnamon, and half a liter of ice-cold *leche deslactosada* she had taken out of the fridge five minutes before.

She picked up the butane lighter she kept on top of a toaster oven under the cabinets next to the sink and lit the left front burner under the saucepan. As soon as the milk started to simmer, she used the long wooden spoon to mix the thick pieces of dark chocolate, the panela, and the milk together. Her whole body moved with the spoon's slow repetition of Xs and Os in the milk as the aroma of hot chocolate filtered up to the ceiling over the stove.

"Hmmmmm, delicious." She closed her eyes, held her hair back, bent her slender body over the saucepan, and breathed in the chocolaty vapor.

She turned the flame of the gas burner down. She picked up the carton of milk, and as she squeezed past, she brushed my lips with the tip of a forefinger. She opened the door of the fridge and placed the milk on the second shelf built into the door.

"Hot chocolate with cheese," she said aloud, then reached in and took out a plate of sliced mozzarella and placed it on the tiled countertop.

She turned, opened the door to the cabinet over the kitchen sink, and took down two white porcelain cups and two saucers from the bottom shelf. She set the saucers and cups on a small tray she had positioned on the kitchen counter next to the range and placed the cups on them, turned off the burner, picked up the saucepan, and poured hot chocolate into each cup.

I think about my cousin every time I look at you and want to make your life better and try to have and make up for what was impossible to have with her.

She indicated the plate of sliced cheese with her chin and picked up the tray.

"Bring the cheese," she said.

I stepped over to the counter, picked up the plate of cheese, and had to turn sideways to pass behind her. As I brushed behind her, she pushed back into me, reached down behind her, and touched me with the fingertips of her left hand.

"Excuse me." She laughed.

I carried the cheese into the dining area of our large living room, set the plate down on the large wooden table, and stood behind my usual chair at the end of the table. She followed me and placed the cups of hot chocolate on the table; I moved around to pull back the chair at the side of the table so she could sit. Two large windows stretched across the wall facing the patio below.

"*Un caballero*," she said, and sat down, "and so nice."

"My father was from Oklahoma—a true southern gentleman," I said. "It's a mistake to confuse being *polite* with being *nice*."

"The Italian was a *gentleman*."

"My point exactly." I laughed. "A married gentleman, if I recall. He wore chartreuse-colored pants, you told me."

"Your accent becomes decidedly more British when you play the role of a gentleman and talk about my ex-boyfriend, the Italian." She laughed. "*Mio fratello italiano*, my Italian brother."

"Must've got the accent from a few pages of a play by Oscar Wilde I read yesterday. Can't remember the name of the play, but the dialogue came fast and furious and was full of mostly trivial English upper-class nonsense. I believe the Italian would prefer to be much more than your '*fratello*.'"

"Oscar made a big impression on your English accent."

"I could use my accent from Oklahoma—the hickified one?" I took a sip of the hot chocolate. "This hot chocolate is marvelous."

"I put cinnamon in it and panela," she said. "I don't understand that word, *hickified*. I always wanted to speak English with a British accent."

"I believe you do. After all of those English classes you took at the British Council, you sound British but with an accent. You speak English with a Colombian Spanish twist." I sipped my hot chocolate and spooned out a string of melted cheese. "Rather charming, so don't change it, if you want my opinion. *Hickified* means like a campesino, country bumpkin, unsophisticated. Like a hick."

"You speak Spanish just like your Spanish teacher," she said.

"My Spanish must have a very feminist sound to it," I said. "Ninety percent of all the Spanish I hear comes from you."

"Yes, you sound and talk just like I do." She laughed. "Your English has a feminine lilt now too. Oscar Wilde might have been more feminine than I."

"Oscar was gay?"

"Yes, *mi amor*, he was. Next, if you're not careful, you'll out yourself, or worse, become a socialist like me." She laughed.

"No, I won't. Truth is, I found out yesterday, I've been an existentialist all my life. Came across the word when reading an article about how the left is losing ground in France. Googled it."

"You're an existentialist, are you?"

"I am. Existentialism is a philosophy I can sink my teeth into and relish. Been one all my life."

"You´re joking, but I am a true socialist," she said seriously.

"Socialism seems irrational to an existentialist like me, but that means you're making progress. At least you're not a communist anymore." I laughed. "You´re married to a gringo, and, if you are not careful, you'll jump into my capitalist pond and learn to swim with sharks."

"I think of gringos more like barracudas." She laughed.

"We existentialists believe people live in a hostile and indifferent world. You, for example, might be a unique and isolated woman, but you do have freedom of choice. However, you must be responsible for the consequences of your actions. You socialists can't be pointing fingers at the government all the time or expecting to be rescued if you choose to live in a flood plain."

"Don't talk for me. I think the government should help people. You remember seeing pictures of all the people on the coast standing in water up to their knees in front of their flooded-out houses. The government did nothing for them."

"Help them help themselves, we existentialists believe." I laughed. "Teach them to fish. Be good to know how with all that water. Different year, same flood, year after year. You ask me, those people love high water."

"Give them fishing poles? That's your answer?"

"Well, yes, tools. Provide an education that teaches rational thinking and good reconstruction techniques would be a good start. You socialists could all pay taxes to use to teach them to build houses on stilts. That sort of thing."

"You don't know what you're talking about."

"Well, that's true, but not knowing what I am talking about doesn't stop me from knowing I am right." I laughed. "Socialists could help by telling their intellectual communist brothers to lay down their arms and stop the senseless war that's been going on for the last fifty years here in Colombia."

"They're not our brothers, but you're right. The war needs to end. It serves no purpose. Peace will help the country move on toward positive things for all Colombians."

"I have an idea that would help. All the leaders of the FARC should volunteer to spend a few years in solitary confinement. Their ignorant followers could be reconciled, or whatever worked down in South Africa. A few years spent meditating in isolation would help the leaders on a path to help their country. Helped that guy who became president of Uruguay, what's his name, Jose Mucica."

"His name is Mujica with a *J*. Sounds like an *H* in English. *Muhica*." She put another small slice of cheese in my hot chocolate.

"That's the guy. He was a rebel leader in Uruguay. He spent ten years in prison. He had a lot of time for reflection. I admire him. I think it would do the leadership of the FARC a lot of good too." I tried another bite of melting cheese. "It's better than I thought it would be. Cheese in hot chocolate!"

"They'd never agree." She gave the dog a slice of cheese.

"Of course they would not agree. They believe it is okay to serve and die for their cause, as long as they don't have to do the dying in the serving."

"You don't understand what happened in Colombia in the seventies and eighties." She gave the dog another slice of cheese, looked at me, and winked. "I like spoiling the animals in my life."

"You do a good job of it. Thanks." I laughed and toasted her with my cup of hot chocolate and cheese.

"Your cousin Dee spoiled you too, I bet," she said.

"Dee was a long time ago, but yes, she was a good spoiler—a good teacher." I laughed.

"What did she teach you?"

"She taught me art. She was an artist. Liked to draw cats, as I recall. She got a job teaching art in public school down in Miami after graduating from Northwestern University up in Chicago—Evanston, Illinois, actually.

"You are still doing your terrible imitation of Oscar's British accent. Did she teach you how to draw cats when you went down to Miami to visit her?"

"More or less. One time, when I was still in high school, she came over to visit us. We lived in a town called Aurora about thirty miles west of Chicago. She showed me how to do pen-and-ink washes. The best part was she fashioned the pen from a small dry tree branch and used it as the pen. I never forgot the trick."

"Did she show you any more tricks?"

"I don't remember." I laughed.

"At least, you did not forget how to draw. I love the pastel drawing you did of me and my cat."

"In the drawing your cat is giving me the evil eye and you are naked. All the tricks I remember now, you taught me."

"So much for the myth about old dogs and new tricks." She laughed.

"I don't know. It *is* Sunday. Maybe we can see how good my memory is later this afternoon."

"There's nothing wrong with your memory." She laughed. "Drink your hot chocolate before it gets cold."

6 Twelve Long Years

"You made coffee?"

"I did. There's milk in the fridge, if you want it. Sugar's on the table. Help yourself."

"All you have is low fat?" He poured a couple of ounces out of the carton into a large white mug with *Baby Doll* in red letters painted at an angle on one side.

"A girl's got to watch her weight." She picked up the coffeepot and filled his cup. "Most guys don't stick around for coffee."

"Most guys?"

"Well...you know."

"You have a lot of guys, do you? I'm not the only one."

"You're the first to complain about low-fat milk." She laughed. "Any other complaints?"

"None I can think of." He sipped the coffee. "Coffee's not bad."

"You weren't bad last night or earlier this morning." She poured some coffee in a mug with *He's My Daddy* in blue script.

"When you're ready for a refill..." he said.

"I'd love it, but I have to go to work."

"It's Saturday." He poured more coffee into his mug. "How come you've got to work?"

"Just for a couple of hours. I'll be back in time for Linda's party. She's looking forward to her birthday party. I can't believe she's twelve years old or that we've been married that long."

"Twelve long years." He laughed, moved close to her, cupped his hand under a small breast, and touched the large nipple with the tip of a finger. "Gorgeous."

"Too bad I have to go to my office." Her hand touched him through the thin cotton of his pajama bottoms. She reached and pulled them down, wrapped her fingers around his penis. She stroked his foreskin back, bent and took him into her mouth. She pulled her mouth away and laughed.

"Don't lose that thought. I'll be back," she said with her Arnold Schwarzenegger Terminator voice, and laughed again.

7 Maybe Tomorrow

"I can't tell the difference."

"You can't tell when I'm acting?" She laughed. "You aren't sure?"

"Do you love me for me?" I said. Sounded weak and stupid to me too.

"You're funny. I must not be a good actress if you don't believe me when I tell you you're the best, and I love you." She laughed again and bit his earlobe. "Maybe you confuse love for lust."

"You are making fun...I don't want to be used—manipulated." What the fuck is happening to me? Shut the fuck up.

"Poor, silly baby. You told me a long time ago, 'Use me, abuse me, and make me like it.'"

"That was a joke...I was joking."

"You didn't mean use and abuse?" She laughed and pulled off her top.

"Seemed like a good idea. You were naked and sitting on top of me."

"*No del todo malo*," she said. "Not all bad. I want you inside me. *Ahora*!"

"Sometimes, even I don't know when I'm acting." She laughed. "When I'm naked and you are...what was the word you used? Manipulating?"

"Manipulating. Yes." She pushed him deep inside of her.

"Yes...there. Oh, baby."

I opened my eyes. Sunlight slashed through the open window and over my face and forced me to throw a forearm across my eyes. After a second, the red haze cleared. I tried again. The sharp brightness filtered between half-opened lids. Silence from the taxi stand on the street two floors below. No radio playing a salsa beat.

The music went on all night, and most of the time, after two months, I slept through the busy dance of humanity below on the street. After 3:00 a.m., the occasional beat of the music filtered into my consciousness—the music...and the fragments of dreams I never quite remembered.

Rum and salsa, a ravaging combo, I thought as I struggled to sit up and untangle the sweat-soaked sheets that tied me to the narrow bed pushed tight up against the outside wall and under the bottom of the warped windowsill.

High on the wall, above the bathroom door, Willy, my roommate, not normally out in daylight, was a muted blue. His color depended on which wall of our room he hung out on: pale yellow, lime green, and this morning, a chalky blue.

Naked, I stumbled my way under and past Willy's roving eyes, leaning over the stool; I braced myself against the wall with both hands and peed into the middle of a rusty circle marking the bottom of the bowl four inches below the rim. I pushed off the wall, flushed, reached in and opened the single valve of the shower, and stepped into the tiled stall. The stream of lukewarm water ran over my head and shoulders, no need for hot water at this latitude.

Five minutes under the water was all I got until it flowed to a trickle. I toweled off and wrapped the towel around my waist. I pushed in close to the cracked mirror over the stained porcelain sink. Puffy circles under dark, bloodshot eyes hooded by thin eyebrows. The shadow of a triangle of loose skin hanging under a chin and thin mouth and a big, too-often-broken nose, all framed by too-long gray hair that stuck out in all directions.

"Not good," the mouth in the face in the mirror mumbled. "Not good today."

Water dripped from the faucet and rinsed the razor in the sink. The cheeks and neck scraped and nicked clean of the two-day growth of gray stubbles with a Schick disposable. Its blade, new twenty shaves ago, did little to revitalize the worn reflection.

"Got to straighten up, son."

Damp hair fingered coarsely down and back, tossing the thin towel over the hook by the shower stall, I padded out of the bathroom. From a wooden bench at the foot of the bed, I picked up, shook out, and stepped into a pair of not-too-dirty jeans I'd left wadded up on top of the bench when I fell naked into bed last night. I pulled my last clean shirt off the rack of a heavy wooden armoire parked on the wall next to the bench.

As I shrugged into the shirt, I searched for and found a pair of socks in the top drawer of the wooden armoire, retrieved my boots kicked under the bed, and sat down on the bed to pull on the socks and boots. Dressed, I got my billfold from under the mattress.

"Coffee time, Willy."

The now-pale-yellow gecko watched as I headed out without locking the door behind me, went down the stairs, through the deserted lobby, and out the front door. A head taller than most of the brown faces crowding the street, I stepped into the hot, bright blue of the day.

The buzz of neon spelled out *H TEL AlAMEDA* above tall wooden doors and followed me into the street. Fifty a week, and the *dueña* did my laundry for another fifteen bucks. She offered to do it for free after the first month. The price turned out to be too high. Easy to understand why her husbands all ran off.

A line of small yellow cars, most of them newer Kias or Chevys, lined the curb along the street. The drivers lounged against their cars' fenders, talking and joking while waiting for a customer or a call.

"Taxi, señor?"

I pointed to the bakery La Panadería Superior a few doors down the street, and he lost interest.

"*El pan fresco saldrá después de las once*, fresh bread will be out after eleven," explained a short, brown-skin girl with a candy-striped apron when she saw me looking at the mostly bare stainless steel shelves along the wall with a sprinkling of small french loaves and other types of bread, the names of which I never remembered.

They need French lessons on how to bake bread: Long, hot, fresh, baguettes.

A patio in the rear of the bakery opened to a cloudless sky. Stainless steel tables topped with coffee cups in front of men and women dressed for business or work in shops. At the back of the patio, a wall fountain splashed water into a narrow pool at its base. On a side wall above the tables, a large flat-screen TV. A beautiful newscaster mouthed the silenced news with subtitles running in Spanish across the bottom of the screen.

You only watch the news because all the presenters are beautiful women, her voice laughed as I moved past.

A different girl in a striped apron followed me to a table I chose near the fountain. I pulled out a chair, sat down with a clear view of the TV, and asked for a *café con leche.*

"*Algo más*, something more?"

"Yes, but you're way too young," I said in English.

"Señor?"

"*Solo el café,* only the coffee," I said.

"You have to move on. A decision has to be made today," the voice in my head said. "You have to stop living in the past."

The coffee arrived.

"Tomorrow," I said aloud.

"Señor?"

"*Nada. Estaba hablando a mí mismo*, thinking out loud."

I took a sip of my *café con leche.*

"*Mañana. Quizás mañana*," I told the light-chocolate steaming liquid in the white cup. "Maybe tomorrow."

8 *Did You Tell Him?*

She stood there looking at him, her face full of loathing. His rage was surging and rippling in every pore of his skin. He wanted to smack her across her arrogant mouth. Close it up forever. God, he wanted to beat the hell out of her, to make her pay. She had her back to the bedroom door. Instead, he drove his fist through the flimsy veneer of the door next to her head.

"Fuck you. Go ahead and kick the door to pieces too while you're at it." She spat at him with disgust.

He stopped himself from doing just that. He wanted to kick the whole cheap trailer to pieces. He'd been out of work for a year. They had to rent the cheapest thing they could find. He hated what he had become—a man defeated, overwhelmed by his feeling of failure and despair. He wanted to slap her taunting mouth off her face.

"God damn it," he said. "God damn it all to hell!"

"God's got nothing to do with nothing, you stupid...what´s the use."

He stepped back. She had been a beauty. *La cosa più bella del mondo*, he'd told her in Italian when making love the first time. That's how he thought of her—the most beautiful thing in the world. He'd loved her so much that he thought the whole weight of the universe would crush his heart when he was not with her. He missed her so much. Now it was all he could do not to kill her, to beat her to a pulp.

"God damn it to hell." He sobbed, shaking his head and pressing his temples with meaty, giant fists as hard as he could.

The black pressure to destroy everything in his path—to strike out and hit and hit—was unbearable. He would never accept how his whole life had gone sour. Losing his job had been the start, but the final straw was her betrayal.

"I am leaving you, Ricardo. It's over. You think beating me up will make me love you, make me want to be with you, stay with you in this pit of a place?"

"I love you," he said. "I'm your husband."

"You're pathetic is what you are. Get out of my way." She reached past him and picked up the scuffed-up suitcase off the bed. She pushed opened the ruined door.

"Don't come near me again," she said. Dragging the suitcase behind her, she left him sitting on the sagging bed. An old pickup was parked and waiting down the cracked street with the engine running. She threw the suitcase in the back, opened the passenger-side door, climbed in, and slammed the door shut behind her.

"Get me out of here."

"Did you tell him?" the blond guy behind the wheel said.

"You better drive on out of here before he comes out of that trailer and you find out firsthand," she said, wiping her tearing eyes with the ragged cuff of her long-sleeved shirt pulled down over her right hand and clenched tightly against her knuckles. She leaned back against the seat and shut her eyes as the truck slipped into gear and moved out.

The park, a trailer trash heap was how she thought of it, and the last of her husband slid away behind the truck's exhaust. This guy's no better, she thought. He's a stepping stone to another… what? She didn't want to think about her future.

"You got any money?" His long, oily, blond hair hung limply down to his shoulders and hid most of his face. She did not answer. She didn't want to look at him, wanted to disappear. She wanted to make him stop the truck, wanted to escape, wanted to run and run until running took her to…fuck, she thought. Escape to where?

"Do you?" he asked again. "We need to stop for gas and get some beer."

"Same crappy deal, different guy," she mumbled.

"What'd you say." The greasy hair fell back from his face when he turned his head and looked at her. He was good looking. Had lead-singer-in-a-rock-band looks but zero talent. His looks had got him plenty of women, but once past the looks, they soon got tired of his constant whiny needs and pettiness. Washed up and didn't know it.

"I said I got twenty bucks." The last twenty you'll see from me, she thought. A long crack in the plastic material ran from the top of the glove box across the top of the dashboard to the base of the front window. Papers and receipts from Walmart were littered in the center console, and the floorboard by her feet was strewn with cartons from McDonalds and Burger King.

She kicked her flip-flops off, pulled her legs up, and tucked her feet under her on the cracked vinyl of the truck's beat-down seat. Saw a Quick Trip coming up on the right. The truck slowed and turned in.

The needle of the gas gauge was riding the red line above empty. He needed a refill as well. A tall Quick Trip sign appeared ahead just ahead of the exit from the interstate. He moved his new, small, expensive RV over to right lane. Best car I've ever owned, he thought. Drives like a car and all the comforts of home where ever I end up.

He pulled into the QuikTrip, parked at a pump, and got out. He slid his credit card through the slot, punched in his zip code, selected regular gas, and lifted the nozzle. When the pump started filling the RV's tank, he walked into the convenience store to use the restroom and to get a coffee.

As he passed the checkout counter, he saw a tall blond woman. A six-pack of Bud Light was on the counter in front of her. She didn't look at him. Her long, slender feet were bare. She didn't look particularly happy, but something alluring about her...he walked passed without speaking to her but wanted to... she's probably married with three kids, he thought as he found the door to the restrooms.

He added too much half-and-half to the dark-roast Colombian coffee, paid the $1.49 to the clerk behind the counter with a twenty dollar bill. He sipped his coffee as he walked through the parking lot to the RV. The next pump over, the blonde was talking to a long-haired guy with his hand inside the handle and pressing the trigger of the pump's nozzle filling up the tank of an old pickup. He watched the guy hang the nozzle back on the pump, turn and look across the top of the pickup at the women with her hand on the door handle of the open passenger-side door.

"Do what the fuck you want. I have places to be," he heard the guy say too loudly. He watched him get into the truck and started the engine.

The woman reached into the back of the truck and pulled out a suitcase, tossed the six-pack onto the passenger seat, slammed the door, and stepped back as the truck moved too fast away from the pumps, made a sharp turn onto the road fronting the stations, and sped away. The whole show didn't take more than half a minute. He finished topping off the tank of the RV and hung the nozzle up. He turned and looked at the woman standing next to her suitcase.

"Looks like you need a ride," he said to her.

The woman turned and looked directly at him. He watched her decide. Without answering, she reached down and picked up her suitcase.

"We thought it was an old Dodge truck backfiring," the old woman said three days later. She had called the police. "I couldn't stand the stink anymore," she told the cop who responded.

The cop went next door and knocked. There was no mistaking the smell. The door was not locked. He went in. The medical examiner placed the time of death at sometime Thursday afternoon.

According to his driver's license, he was a forty-three-year-old named Ricardo Santini from Miami. He had shot himself on his birthday, but no one thought to put that fact down in the report. The report mentioned scars over his eyebrows and a tattoo with the name Evelyn. The word *Forever* written underneath the name.

"I think the wife run off," the old woman told the cops without being asked. She stood in the street dressed in a blue housecoat missing all but one button. Her feet stuffed in a pair of dirty, rundown house shoes below swollen ankles and stockings rolled down past her knees.

An old, scrawny man with a potbelly stood beside her. He had a rash that ran up his right arm and disappeared into the short sleeve of his soiled, limp white shirt. A thin fuzz did little to cover his pink scabby scalp.

"The wife was a looker—a beauty," the old man added. "Eyetalian she was. Didn't have much to do with folks. Weren't from around here. She was a looker."

"You was the *looker*," the old woman said. "You was the one trying to get a look all the time. The husband was the '*Eyetalian*,' not the wife. Of course, I didn't pay much attention."

"She was a looker," the old man repeated under his breath as he scratched with dirty, broken fingernails at the angry red rash that escaped out the stained, frayed neck of his shirt, ran up the side of his neck, and disappeared behind a hairy ear.

"A real good looker. Eyetalian," he repeated.

9 Please

The huge face the size of a full moon peaks over the mountain. Petrifying bloodshot eyes in that orange balloon face look down at me. Never a monster in the closet or under the bed for me.

When did the face start? I don't remember, but it is not only lurking somewhere in my subconscious. The face is too real for that.

Oh, the face is not as terrifying today as it was sixty-five years ago. Today, the face is not as well defined as it was for a five-year-old, but the eyes in that face still penetrate to my most unforgiving secrets. The eyes see into me and understand what kind of man that boy I was became. The eyes accuse. The eyes are unforgiving.

We share only ten or twelve truly terrible secrets, the face and I. The mouth in that face hides behind the mountain. Hidden, I can't see the mouth screaming all the truths about me. I know what the merciless mouth would scream if I could see it. My hands under the covers would be helpless to cover the face's mouth and stop it from screaming my secrets. Everyone would know!

For seventy-four years, I've been lucky. Only the orangey hair and the mocking red-glowing eyes of the face are visible, but that is enough. I squeeze shut my eyes tight, but no matter. The face grows largest at midnight. No!

Please do not let the monster that owns that face rise up on its hind legs and leap across the mountain.

Please don't. Please...

10 Blessed

The piercing bluish light that flooded the room and washed away all color had no visible source.

The chair's steel frame cut red marks into the man's back and held the man upright in front of a steel desk also bolted to the floor. The man's skin hung loose about his body. His feet were long and dirty, yellow nails broken.

A woman sat behind the desk. A long, flowing hooded robe hid her face; the wide sleeves of the robe pulled back. The skin of the back of her hands and arms was translucent with veins snaking up and disappearing into the sleeves of her robe. An improbable shadow extended across the top of the desk and ran up to but did not touch the bound white naked form in front of the desk.

"Do you believe in the Holy Ghost?" the woman demanded.

"No," he whispered with a painful shake of head.

"God?"

"No." Louder.

"You don't believe in the spirit and the afterlife?"

"No. Lies that are inexplicable and outside of reason." The man's eyes flamed.

"A God-fearing atheist!" the shadowed voice accused.

"No. I do not fear God. I fear the ignorant who do believe and the lies that control their lives. Hideous and terrible acts committed in the name of their beliefs. The hordes of humanity lost to their beliefs."

"May God have mercy!" she shouted, and raised her fat-fingered right hand high. The sleeve of her robe fell to her shoulder, exposing old and faded symbols tattooed around her bloated bicep.

"I hear the call to battle between irrational and rational forces. Battles fought by generations after generations and eternally lost!"

"You hear his voice, his almighty voice!" Her voice high pitched.

"Never! I hear the voice of sanity scratching, whispering in my head, the voice of reason deep inside me."

"Blasphemy!" The woman's voice filled the blue light with indignation.

"Truth!" The last of his energy expended, he slumped against the cruel cords that bound him to the chair.

A tall, thin shadow moved from the wall behind the bound man. Dressed in a vintage too-large-and-worn shiny black suit, white shirt buttoned snug to his neck, his feet in black wing-tipped dress shoes with heavy leather soles, a thin, young man steps forward. With one swift motion, he buried an ice pick up to the base of the handle into the right ear of the naked man.

The naked man went ridged with surprise and collapsed back into his bonds. There was only a trickle of blood. A thin red line ran down the neck. A yellow pool slowly formed under the chair.

"Oh, Daddy!"

The woman rose, walked around the desk, embraced and joined hands with the young man. They left the room together holding hands. At the door they looked back at the naked shrunken form in the chair. They embraced and kissed. A tongue searched deep in a hot, moist mouth and withdrew.

"Oh, Mother!"

The woman's robe opened. Her large blue-veined breasts hung down against the rolls of fat around her belly. Hungry, thin white fingers plunged between huge thighs.

A hand reached out, pushed the door shut, and killed the murderous brightness of the bluish light. The blackness was total. All or nothing may be false or everything true. In that complete darkness, the young man pushed deep inside the most beautiful women of his dreams. Consecrated desire filled the dark with certainty in the narrow black hallway.

"Oh, Sweet Baby Jesus!"

11 Scuffling

From behind the bar, I could see everything that was going on in the place. I stood and watched Sammy fucking up. He sat at a table more than six or seven feet from where I was standing. He was with his bud, Chink. He was drinking bourbon and Coke and flipping cigarette butts at a tall, thin guy wearing a cowboy hat and sitting at another table with his back turned toward him. It would be only a matter of minutes before the cowboy figured out what was going on. Then, we would have us a show.

I didn't know why I still permitted Sammy to drink in my bar. He was always causing trouble. Maybe I was bored, or maybe I liked trouble. I'd barred him out of the place a few times but always let him back in. I watched Sammy flip a butt that hit the cowboy square on the back of the neck. I moved toward the end of the bar so I could step out and bust up the scuffle that was about to start.

The kid I had working with me behind the bar had been watching too. He was the son of one of my customers. He was a bit overweight. Good hearted. Everybody liked him.

"Look. See what Sammy's doing?"

He shook his head and shrugged. He didn't understand why I let the stuff that Sammy was always pulling go on. I shrugged back to say, me neither. I saw that the cowboy was in Sammy's face and had him by the lapels of his leather jacket.

"I'll be right back," I told the kid. I stepped out and took a couple of steps over to the two new best friends. I pushed between the cowboy and Sammy and pulled Sammy toward the door.

I manhandled him outside and pushed him up against the side of the building to the right of the door. He was drunk. I stepped back and told him he had to go home.

"You telling me to leave?" he said.

"Time to go," I told him.

"You telling me to leave?" he repeated.

His buddy, Chink, was standing outside off to the side but had not butted in. When I turned my head and looked at him to make sure he understood to stay out of it, Sammy hit me in the mouth.

Chink was shocked. I don't think Sammy believed he'd done it either, but he didn't have more than a split second to reflect on his mistake.

I caught Sammy across the face with my forearm and knocked his head against the concrete block wall of the building. He melted down the wall like hot butter.

Chink moved over and covered him so I would not hit him again. I helped Chink pick him up and carry him to Chink's old pickup.

When I went back inside and walked back behind the bar, the kid gave me an I-told-you-so look. He wrapped up a handful of ice in a bar rag and handed it to me. I pressed it against my cut lip.

"Sammy going to live?" he wanted to know.

"Depends on how hard the idiot's head is," I said, and pressed the cold, damp bar rag tight against my lip. "I underestimated how long Sammy's arm was. I'll know better next time."

"Fuck, next times," he said.

The kid shook his head in disgust. He finished pouring orange juice into a seven-ounce pony glass full of ice and a shot of vodka. Walked to the end of the bar and placed the screwdriver on a clean bar napkin in front of a regular customer.

"You ought to bar that fucking Sammy," the guy said, toasting me with his new cocktail. "He's a fuckup, and you know it. He's nothing but trouble."

"Thanks for the tip," I said through the ball of bar towel filled with ice pressed against my lip, wishing I'd measured the length of Sammy's arm better.

"I will next time for sure," I mumbled into the bloody wet cloth.

12 *Soon*

Now, he thought about it all the time. When he would do it? When he'd decide? When he'd check out, about when his disgust and frustration would make him decide to end it, to say to the world, "no more."

"After a while, a guy starts thinking it ain't worth the effort," he thought aloud.

He walked the beach. As far as his eyes could see, white sand with cracked shells that bruised his bare feet. Old people walked ahead of him and followed behind.

"We're a fucking parade," he thought. "A parade of dry, wrinkled, sunburnt skin and flaccid muscles."

He was tired of looking at turkey-necked men with their bellies hanging down over their shorts and women with tits no longer fighting gravity.

"Dried up old prunes, all of us. Jesus!"

He looked down when he was pissing and couldn't see his dick. Even when he woke up with a hard on, he couldn't see the fucker hidden behind the mountain of his belly. For Christ's sake, he had to push himself up and off the bed with his arms when he stood up in the middle of the night and stumbled into the toilet to pee.

His wife was old and tired, a lunatic lost in a head full of the past. He no longer saw her as the young bride he'd married fifty years ago. He saw her as she was now and hated her for her insecurities and the same questions repeated every five fucking minutes. She would not give him a minute's peace. Jesus!

"Armond!" she shouted. "Armond!"

He heard her searching room to room.

"It won't be long before she finds me again," he said to himself. "Jesus Christ in a handbasket!"

"There you are," she said. "The children will be here soon."

His son had died crashing his motorcycle twenty years ago. The daughter was in California. She would not be coming anytime soon. Had refused to come home since her mother disowned her twenty years ago after she'd married the Spic. He had not approved of Raul neither. Jesus! Son of a bitch proved him wrong: owns one of the largest construction companies in Northern California.

Today, the old guy from Meals on Wheels who brought lunch three days a week would be by in an hour. After lunch, he could escape again to the beach that ran in front of his modest house. The hired woman could fill in for a couple of hours. His wife called her Eunice.

"Eunice!" she shouted every five minutes. "Oh, my beautiful child, my lovely daughter, you are home at last."

Every day, when he comes home from the beach, he checks his stash, his hidden escape plan of fifty pills—the strongest pills available. The directions said take one for a full night's sleep and no more than two every twenty-four hours.

Today when he held the bottle of pills in his hand, he was tempted.

"Now," the voice in his head told him. "Do it now!"

"No, but soon," he told the voice. "Soon."

13 House Rules

He had stopped taking baths, washing his hair, or cleaning himself up. No reason to, and he wasn't going to do it. He lived alone. His young wife, the only thing he'd ever loved, or cared about, was gone. He didn't blame *her*. It was not her fault. He knew whose fault it was all right. He wanted to kill the bastard, boil him alive, strip every inch of skin from his body with a pair of needle-nose pliers.

"I'm going to ride my bicycle over to the market and get some milk and eggs," she'd said. "I'll get you a surprise for breakfast too."

She'd kissed him on her way out of the house. He'd never seen her alive again. Drunk driver, the police said. They had caught the bastard and hauled his ass to jail before he could get to him.

Bottom line was he was alone. They had had no children. The two of them had been enough—all they needed. Two days ago, he'd decided. No bathing was the new house rule—the new policy.

Months ago, he'd cleaned out the place by either throwing everything away or giving it away. He had lost the most important part of himself. His wife was now buried treasure. He'd let church people haul off a lot of his stuff, take away all that represented a lifetime of his work in the oil fields of so many foreign countries. He'd had to learn how to say, "I don't speak your language" ten different ways.

He liked the new pretend-freedom the empty house gave him. He had a chair, kept a cot and a small table for food and drink. The kitchen was intact, but the fridge was mostly empty, like the rest of the house. Now, if he could get rid of the memories, big and small, trapped in his head.

He remembered one time a young woman telling him, "You don't smell old like most old men do." Another time, a young hairdresser said, "You're not as repulsive as a lot of old guys."

She didn't say *repulsive*, but he couldn't remember the exact word she'd used. When she'd said it, he had been occupied looking in the mirror at the skin under his chin hanging over the edge of the cover she had thrown over him and tightened around his neck to keep the cuttings from his thin, gray hair from falling on his shirt and pants.

He wished he could remember the word she'd used. He never went back to her for a haircut after she'd said it. He had been thinking that plastic surgery might be in his future just before she said it.

He had accumulated a whole bunch of "never-going-backs" over the years. The list would fill a ream of paper, if he cared to write it down, which he'd been thinking about doing. Maybe he would make a story up for each one. He could paper his empty house with the stories. Fill up the house with the furnishings from his mind now that he had made space.

He would throw stuff out of his mind as he'd done with all the crap that had filled up his house. He would purge his head of all he knew—all his mistakes, words he wished he could take back, faces of old girlfriends whose names he couldn't remember, memories of dark women in hot, dry countries.

He would write it all down. Someday, perhaps he could write about the last kiss. The nights of madness that followed, his anger. Yeah, he would write it all down.

No. He might purge the anger from his memories, but never the last kiss. He would not write about the last kiss. He'd hold on to the memory of the last kiss. Hold on until his last breath.

But one thing was for certain. From now on, he would follow the new house rules: no more baths. He'd write his stories and smell like an old man. What was that word the hairdresser had used? Never mind. No more haircuts neither!

14 The Portrait

Today, I drew a self-portrait. It was a simple line drawing with charcoal pencil. To draw the portrait, I used a mirror with a crack running through the upper left corner.

I leaned the mirror up against some books placed in front of my drawing tablet resting on a small easel on the dining room table. I faced a large picture window. The natural and harsh light that flooded my face hid and disguised nothing.

I drew the portrait quickly without thinking and without erasures. I was surprised that I had not distorted the proportions of my face in my usual fashion of drawing a face with one side shorter than the other side—most of my portraits looked lopsided. Maybe the crack in the mirror helped me keep it straight.

The thing that I had not counted on was how wrinkled and sagged my face had become. How could I have not noticed? I shaved my jaw every morning.

The portrait was true—hateful. The skin under the chin was loose and drooped. The neck was not fat, but the skin hung down and formed a triangle running into the shirt collar. The nose had deep pores and was larger than I remembered. Under the eyes were dark circles, and there were wrinkles radiating from the corners, but perhaps not from laughing too much.

The forehead was exaggerated in the drawing too, or had the hair receded that much? How could that be? The hair was thinner too. Where did that brooding look come from? Who was this man whose face I had sketched?

I did not want to accept the truth of my work—the facts so plainly clear in the portrait. I had drawn an old man. The man everyone sees but no one I recognized. I wanted to tear the paper, to shred it, to bury in the trash the truth drawn so meanly—the truth I had become.

15 The Sketch

He met the woman on the internet through a dating service. He had looked at a hundred photos and read an equal number of profiles. Finally, he'd emailed a brown-haired woman who wrote in her profile that she liked sailing and hiking and wanted to meet someone who was into outdoor activities. She had posted five photos and looked to be tall and rangy.

She emailed him back. They hooked up on Skype and chatted. He found out she was divorced and an artist too. Most of the time when they chatted online, she sat at a table in her dining room with her back to a wall hung with some of her paintings. She had her favorites framed and hung all over her house, she told him. He invited her to look at his artwork on his website. His were mostly digital paintings of nude women, while her paintings were watercolors of landscapes and flowers.

They enjoyed each other's company online. After a couple of months, they agreed to meet for coffee. She suggested a Starbucks not too far from his house. They met on a Saturday afternoon. She arrived late, but he didn't mind, because he had his computer. He saw her come in. She hesitated just inside the doorway, and he got up and went to where she stood.

They walked together to the counter. She ordered an iced coffee and refused to let him pay. She was in a pair of black jeans, wore a loose sweater and cowboy boots. He had on a brown leather jacket and some gray slacks. He had worn a pair of boat shoes.

A stark contrast to his beautiful Colombian ex-wife, who always used eyeliner at least, she'd used only a light-pink lipstick.

Nor was there a hint of sexuality in the way she was dressed. I wonder if it is on purpose, he thought. *Vamos a ver*, we'll see.

He guided her back to the table where he had left his coffee and laptop, held out a chair for her, moved around the table, and sat down facing her with his back to the wall. He closed the lid of his laptop and pushed it to one side.

They both took a sip of their drinks. He reached into his briefcase and pulled out a drawing pad and a charcoal pencil. He started sketching her portrait. I can't wait to see how we end up. It can go several different ways.

"I loved your paintings," she said. "I thought I wouldn't."

"We are both artists," he said, thinking, you don't have to be a good one to be one.

"Yesterday, I asked my pastor to look at your website. He said your paintings were obscene," she said.

"Obscene?"

"Yes, he told me that I had to be careful. Men with an obsession with sex and naked women were sick and dangerous."

"You came anyway."

"I almost stayed away, but I loved your paintings," she said. "I imagined myself posing for you."

He turned the sketch around and pushed it toward her. She looked at it for a long moment and then looked up at him.

"May I keep it?" she said. "It's beautiful."

He nodded yes and took a sip of his coffee.

"You're not dangerous, are you? You won't take advantage of me if I pose naked?" Her eyes were bright and her cheeks faintly flushed.

He reached across the table and lightly caressed a circle on the back of her hand with the tip of a manicured and square-cut nail. She didn't move her hand away.

"No, I won't take advantage." He smiled and thought, "*Al menos no mucho,* at least not much."

16 A Good Monster

I'll bet you a dollar that their grandchildren love dictators who are monsters. You know the ones that rule their countries with an iron fist. We never think of these monsters that use secret police to spy on citizens, or worse, to jail political opponents or to disappear young students and mothers who protest as being beloved grandparents. It's hard to accept that a monster could have loving grandkids, but I bet they do. What do children know?

Dictators are not the only monsters neither. You remember reading about that guy who kept his kid in a cellar? He looked like a regular guy. Like a bus driver or some kind of guy you see but don't see every day.

You remember he had a dungeon-like cellar chamber in Austria where he held his daughter captive for twenty-four years. Josef Fritzl, I remember, was his name. Son of a bitch fathered seven children with her down in that dungeon. I think she was eighteen when her father abducted her and hauled her down there. When I read about what that Fritzl did, I wanted to put my hands on the fucker; made me want to do stuff to him that hurt—bad stuff.

I cannot imagine what kind of monster rapes his kid and keeps her prisoner in a cellar under his house, throwing birthday parties for the daughters born of his crime? You think he baked cakes and lit candles for their birthdays? You think they lived in the big house and went to school while his daughter was naked and hungry and locked up down in that Fritzl guy's cellar? Would the kids he had with his daughter love him like a father, a grandfather, or like some kind old uncle?

You think his daughter's daughters sitting down to breakfast and happily eating cornflakes ever morning knew they might end up celebrating their eighteenth birthday in the cellar tied up next to their mom someday? I bet his older daughter and mother of this new bunch of daughters enjoyed cornflakes until the morning her monster dad hauled her down to the cellar, tied her up naked to the cot, and raped her and locked her in. What kind of monster does that to his own eighteen-year-old kid or grandkid?

My grandmother used to read the paper and weep when she read about some young woman, or child, or anyone who got mistreated, harmed, or died. You think Zula, my grandmother, ever thought about killing the person responsible? No, she did not. She just wiped the tears from her eyes and told us kids all about it. She did not have a bad bone in her body, my grandmother didn't.

Unlike my grandmother, I read about things that bad people do to others in the paper, and it makes me want to kill the child-molesting bastards, the murderers, and the torturers of little kids and women. I read about dictators, and it makes me want to kill those bastards too. What kind of a guy thinks about killing after reading a story in the paper?

You think I might be a monster too? Well, maybe, but if I am, I think I'm a good monster. I don't believe thinking about killing dictators and child molesters makes me a bad monster.

No, I don't think I'm a bad monster at all. Do you? I don't think that 'cause I want to kill a bunch of horrible monsters makes me a bad monster…no, I'm not at all like them other monsters.

If I am a monster, at least I think I'm a good monster.

17 Count on It

The alarm is set for five o'clock in the morning, but I always wake up at a quarter till. Still dark, but in Bogotá, Colombia, daylight comes within seconds of the same time each morning, 365 days a year. There is no change of seasons in Colombia. When I wake up, after I spend a minute thinking about how lucky I am, I throw the covers back, slide out of bed, and pad my way to the bathroom.

No need to turn on the light, I pee leaning over the stool with one hand supporting me against the back wall of the bathroom. I hear rather than see that I hit the target, shake out the last drop, and flush. I step left and bend over the sink, feel for the tap, run cold water over my hands, and splash some onto my face. I feel for the towel hanging to the right of the sink and use it to dry my face and hands.

Before I hear the alarm go off, I make my way back to the bedroom to stop it from buzzing. I want to fall back into bed next to the warm form sleeping under the covers but turn and wade back toward the galley kitchen just a few steps away. I flip on the light over the counter and cover my eyes. I open my fingers slowly to give my eyes a chance to adjust to the glare.

The coffee is Colombian and a dark roast. I spoon five tablespoons full of the fine ground coffee into the Mister Coffee, fill the reservoir with five cups of cold water, and punch the on button. I take a liter of milk out of the fridge and fill my large white porcelain cup half-full, put the cup into the microwave, set it for one minute and twenty seconds, and push start.

The bell dings, and I take the cup of hot milk out of the microwave. I find the pot of sugar and stir in a heaping spoonful of the brown sugar. The coffee is almost done, but I don't wait. I pull the coffeepot and push my cup under the dripping coffee. I tip the pot, fill the cup, and quickly exchange pot for cup.

After a quick stir, I take the day´s first sip of café con leche. A new day, like all my days in Colombia, has begun. I carry my cup of coffee into the dining room and look out the window at the gray light as it comes over the mountains surrounding the city to the east.

The dog was asleep on the couch, but she opens her eyes, and I see her watching me. I sip my coffee. She stretches and pulls herself off the couch and pads to the apartment´s door. I walk over and open the door. She hesitates before she goes out and down the circular staircase to the garden and yard three floors down. I shut the door, walk to the couch, and sit down in front of the fireplace. I take the remote control and push start. The gas logs ignite, and it will only take a few moments to dissipate the night's chill from the apartment.

I get up, open the door, and let the dog in. She follows me into the kitchen. I get her some food and pour it into her bowl. I pour more milk and sugar into my cup and microwave it. I fill the cup to the brim with coffee. When I finish my second cup of coffee, it will be full daylight outside, and I will be ready to shower, dress, and start another day in Bogotá. I like living in Colombia. I like the sameness. I can count on it.

18 The Third World

I sat down in a booth to have breakfast at a local restaurant. A guy I knew slightly nicknamed Bronc stopped by the table to say hello. I pointed at the booth opposite to invite him to join me. Both of us ordered soft scrambled eggs, whole-wheat toast, and bacon—mine with a side of well-done hash browns.

"Been a while," I said. "How ya doing?"

"I ain't dead yet. Still kick'n'," he said.

"I guess you can prove it." I laughed.

"Hell yes. I'm not like all these old guys you see around here. I got myself on an airplane and flew off to South America last year."

The waitress brought two big mugs of coffee.

"I got me a new, young wife and live in Colombia part of the time. I liked the idea of taking risk and setting foot into unknown territories. Sometimes, new places have a lot to offer an old guy. I've never feared starting over, leaving all my stuff behind, and striking out headed for something new, but moving to Colombia was a stretch even for me."

"You got a Colombian wife?"

"Did," he said, and took a big swallow of his black coffee.

"How's that working out?"

"See for yourself."

He pulled out his billfold and took out a creased photo. The woman was young and beautiful with long black hair and large almond-shaped eyes. Could have been a photo of a model he'd cut out of a magazine. She looked familiar.

He winked and put the photo back in his billfold.

Breakfast arrived. I took the cap off the pepper shaker. Covered part of the top of the shaker with my thumb and sprinkled my eggs and hash browns with a liberal dose of pepper, added some salt. Bronc did the same, but not so much pepper.

"One of the biggest reasons I like Colombia is you can walk into any drugstore and buy most drugs without a doctor's script. I've got Glaucoma and have to put a drop of Lumigan in each eye every day for the rest of my life. In the USA, I have to go pay an eye doc to do an exam and write me a prescription at least once a year. In Colombia, if a guy knows the name of the drug he needs, he can buy it, no middleman needed. Viagra especially." He winked again around a mouth full of eggs and bacon.

"That's sounds pretty convenient," I said, and shook a couple of drops of Louisiana Hot Sauce onto my scrambled eggs.

"We don't need no government yahoos to protect us ignorant cowboys," he continued. "We got to take responsibility for our own health. Learn to read about all the side effects before swallowing a damned pill or getting an injection. Got to make educated choices about what we put into our bodies, and those decisions don't need to be made by big government and multinational companies," he said, making more sense than I'd thought him capable of doing.

"We Americans have given up on thinking for our own selves. Look at the result. We are the richest, most overweight, and unhealthiest nation on the planet. Uncle Sam's been bought by big business. Sugar is killing us," he said, and spread a bunch of high-fructose strawberry jam on a triangle of his whole-wheat toast.

"We all could stand to get in shape and lose some weight," I said, looking down at my belly and then over at my breakfast partner. Looked like he needed to get after a bunch of push-ups and sit-ups more than I did, especially him being married to that young hot Colombian. Maybe beautiful Colombians liked fat old gringos. Photo might've been legit. I hoped it was.

"I get a Social Security check every month. Gives me about half the money I need to live a simple life. Oh, I know. It don't sound like living in Bogotá, Colombia, and traveling back to Oklahoma to work from time to time is very simple. Don't matter I'm in Colombia or Oklahoma, my life's pretty much the same."

"Does seem simple." I laughed. He spread more jam on his other piece of toast.

"Well, maybe not as simple as it looks, but at least after three years, I can compare the two worlds with some authority. Big plus is cost of living in Colombia's a lot cheaper than here."

"Cheaper?" I said, interested. I scraped some grape jelly on a piece of dry whole-wheat toast. All the little tubs of strawberry jam, my favorite, Bronc had used up.

"Sure. Drugs, for example, not the illegal kind, if you know what I mean. Drugs are at least fifty percent cheaper, and you don't need to see a doc to get them neither. Food's cheaper and healthier, fresher too. Of course, I'm talking about vegetables and fruit mostly. You can go to fancy, big supermarkets and buy imported food and pay through the nose, but every neighborhood has fruit and vegetable markets, meat markets, you-name-it markets where a guy can buy stuff cheaper."

"I might have to marry me one of those hot Colombians like you did and move down there," I said, mixing some of my hash browns into my scrambled eggs and taking a bite.

"Well, not everything is cheap in Colombia. Don't buy electronics. Almost anything imported you plug into a wall socket is more expensive. Everything imported costs more. Imported cars? Forget about 'em. Cost a third more in Colombia because of the damned import taxes."

"So you have to bring electronics in from the States?" I said, and washed my egg-hash-brown combo down with a big sip of black coffee. I'd been off of the cream and sugar for about a week.

"You got it. The government is screwing everyone, and the country is extremely inefficient, but if you don't have to dick around with trying to make a living in the country and can afford to live in a safe neighborhood, Colombia has some very good parts. And the most beautiful women in the world."

"The most beautiful women? Like your wife?" I looked at him to see if I could tell if he was lying about the woman in the photo. Felt a little jealous. Where had I seen her before?

"Well, you have to be able to afford to play. Pay the rent, if you know what I mean. The prettier she is, the higher the maintenance fees." He laughed. "You can get everything in Colombia, and it's cheaper to rent than to own, if you know what I mean. You know, you don't have to get married necessarily. Don't have to own."

"You don't have to own? Have to get married?"

"No. You can rent." He laughed and winked.

"Are you talking about...?"

"Women!" he finished for me. "It's legal in Colombia."

"You mean prosti—"

"*Prepagos.* They call 'em prepagos in Colombia," he explained.

"But you're married?" I said. Seemed to me I *had* seen his "wife" in one of them women's magazines. One lying around in the place where I got my hair cut. I'd pick it up by accident, but maybe all Colombian women look alike.

"My wife's the one who's married." He laughed.

"Well, if I had a beautiful woman like yours, I don't think I'd have time for a...what did you call them...a prepago, but I'm glad it's legal," I said, and took another sip of my weak coffee. Sugar and cream would have made it better.

"A woman should do as she pleases with her body, you ask me. Me too." He laughed. "Oh, lots of folks complain about exploitation of women and pornography and all that business, but still, I should be able to have a little fun with a pretty young woman when I want to. After all, I won't take all that much of her time or hurt her none. I'm mostly all talk." He laughed again and pushed a big forkful of his scrambled eggs into his mouth.

"Well, I don't know. I am not married, but still..."

"Same thing with marijuana," he said, chewing and talking with his mouth full of eggs. "I like the idea of legalized marijuana. I don't smoke it and don't intend to smoke it, but if I did want to, I think I should be able to walk into a drugstore or supermarket, buy a pack of marijuana, and light up. They just legalized marijuana in Uruguay. I don't know about buying meds without a prescription down there or if prostitution is legal in Uruguay or not. I'll have to check it out."

"Uruguay?" I said, and pushed my plate of half-eaten breakfast to one side.

"More coffee?" one of the older waitresses asked. I started to tell her no, but she filled both our mugs without waiting for an answer.

"Yeah. I'm thinking about hiking on down to Uruguay and looking that place over. Colombia is okay. Uruguay might just be the ticket. Whole country has about same population as Oklahoma.

"That's small," I said.

"Yeah. About the same number of cows too." He laughed. "The capital, Montevideo, is only about a million and got lots of water to play on: the Atlantic Ocean and a big river. But it's a hell of a hike from Oklahoma. All the way down to the bottom of South America. I do know the women are beautiful down there too. I seen pictures. More European looking than in Colombia. Like I said, I ain't dead yet and still have some kick left in me."

"Well, it was good seeing you again, Bronc," I told him, taking a sip of the now-too-hot-to-drink coffee and almost burning my tongue. I picked up both tickets and put a couple of bucks down on the table for a tip as I slid out of the booth.

"I hate to run, but I got to get to work."

"Hey, it was good talking with you. Thanks for breakfast. Get yourself on down to Colombia. Food's great," he said.

"I might just do that. Or Uruguay," I said. "Get me a hot one like yours."

"You bet. Most beautiful women in the world down there. The rent ain't bad neither." He laughed.

I finished paying our tabs up at the register and looked back at Bronc. He turned in the booth and saluted me with his mug of coffee. I waved back and pushed out the door thinking about Colombia, the most beautiful women in the world, and the cost of renting.

19 The Big Tube

My brother laid out the size and shape of the building for his new bar by scratching out the outline of the building in the dirt with a garden hoe.

As soon as the outline was complete, he called a concrete company, and at nine o'clock the next morning, some men came out with a backhoe and a bulldozer and gouged out the foundation.

Two days later, a plumber came out and ran white plastic pipe for the bathroom and bar drains and water lines. He finished thirty minutes before the concrete trucks arrived.

Next day, me and my brother walked all over the hard, smooth, gray concrete.

"Looks bigger 'n I thought it would without the walls up," he said. It *was* big, even after the walls went up.

Two months after the place opened up for business, I walked in on a Saturday night two weeks before Christmas. The entrance to the place was on the lower level, where the pool tables were, and the boss, my brother's wife, was by the door sitting on a folding chair with a money box on a card table and collecting the cover charge for the band. She stood, came around the table, kissed me on the mouth, and slipped me a brass knuckle.

"There's a bunch of drunken idiots in here tonight. I'm expecting trouble," she said.

Drunken idiots were no big exception in the Big Tube Club. That summed up 90 percent of the club's customers, maybe 100 percent if you counted the club's owners and their relatives, me included—especially me. I slipped the brass knuckles in a front pocket of my Wranglers and made my way to the bar on the second level. I ordered a fortifier to get ready for the predicted trouble.

My little brother coined the phrase "big tube" to describe girls who were a lot more than slightly overweight. As a joke, my brother's wife decided Big Tube was a perfect name for the club.

Tonight, the club was full of its namesakes stuffed into jeans two sizes too small, which did nothing to hide how big their butts were. Didn't matter much. The lights of the club dimmed low played an important slimming role, but best beautifier was whiskey poured into seven-ounce pony glasses by the quick hands of the bartenders who worked behind the long bar that stretched along the north wall on the second level.

Several shots of whiskey turned the women beautiful in the men's drunken eyes and saved the girls from expensive cosmetic surgery and having to give up eating double helpings of chicken fried steak and mash potatoes.

The band stepped out and struck a chord at ten o'clock. A trickle of cowboy-booted hombres escorted their partners to the dance floor fronting the bandstand set up across from the bar.

By midnight, everyone was as drunk as they intended to get, and no ugly people were in the house. The dance floor was overflowing with couples bucking and sawing offbeat to the country music blasting from the stage. As drunk as most of the women were, even I might have a chance at getting lucky.

Around twelve thirty, my brother and I were standing at the edge of the second level, looking over the action two steps below us. The crack of cue balls breaking racks of solid and striped balls, and quarters dropping into the coin boxes of the six pool tables on the first level, were music to our ears. A big group of men in denim work shirts, from a local electrical company, were playing dollar-a-game eight ball against a bunch of oil-field hands all wearing white shirts with the logo of an oil-field service company whose owner had arranged a Christmas party for his whole crew.

"I bet it don't last another twenty minutes without a fight," my brother said.

"Ten bucks says you're right." I laughed.

A big fat guy in a white shirt swung his pool cue and hit a tall electrician in denim and wearing a cowboy hat across the back of his head, knocking the hat flying like a Frisbee. The war between blue and white was on.

Between, on top, and under the pool tables began a frenzy of sweaty stopping, punching, and arm-twisting. Didn't mattered much who was fighting with whom or why. Everyone joined in the free-for-all, but with not too much harmful effect.

"Let's give 'em a minute to wear themselves out, and then we'll break their party up," my brother said.

"I owe you ten bucks." I laughed and reached into my pocket and slipped the brass knucks over the knuckles of my right hand.

I picked out the tubby who had started the trouble, stepped down into the action, and threaded my way over to where he was trying to stomp on a guy's head. Tapping him with the brass knuckles on his collarbone to get his attention, I reached in, got ahold of his right hand, and applied a wristlock.

When I bent his wrist and applied serious pressure, he stopped stomping and hitting. The pain in his wrist lifted him up onto his toes and changed his focus.

"You hit me, I'll break your wrist," I told him in a low, calming voice. "Please come with me."

I forced him out of the fray and pulled him over to a row of built-in bench seats running the length of the wall facing the ends of the pool tables. We sat down together like a happy couple, but I kept putting pressure on his wrist with the wristlock so he could concentrate.

"What'd I do?" my new best friend wanted to know. "You're breaking my wrist."

"Yes, I know," I said. "Not so funny now, is it? Let's sit here and enjoy our time-out together."

"I'm going to whip your ass," he said, and tried to pull away and stand up. I applied more pressure on his wrist, sweat broke out on his brow, and he got still again.

"No, you won't," I said, my voice just above a whisper. The band played a new song by Johnny Cash that reminded me of an ex-girlfriend.

I fell into a burning ring of fire.
I went down, down, down,
and the flames went higher.
And it burns, burns, burns,
The ring of fire,
The ring of fire.

"I love Johnny's new song, don't you?" I said to my new buddy as the band ended the second verse. "You ready to be civilized and rejoin the party?"

"Yes, sir."

"Come on. Let's go up to the bar," I said. "I'll buy you a drink."

I released my grip on his wrist and stood. The other warriors were shaking hands, clapping each other on the back, and buying new drinks to replace the ones spilled in the ruckus. I winked at my brother as we walked past.

"Drink up, boys," I heard him say. "Only two more hours till closing time."

20 *Sunday Afternoons*

"*Me gusta estar sola*," she said. "I like being alone."

"Alone?" He repeated. "*Sola*?"

"Yes," she said. "I really like being alone. I don't want to live with someone *todo el tiempo*, all the time."

They were sitting together on a sofa in the living room of her one-bedroom apartment in Bogotá, Colombia. The sofa was white and new but already showed signs of her cat's claws.

"So, you don't want to get married?"

"I do, but I don't." She laughed. "Can you understand what I mean?"

"I can." He looked at her and smiled. "You want your own space, a private place that belongs just to you."

"Yes. If we got married, I might like to live in separate houses, or apartments," she said. "Does that sound selfish?"

"Yes." He laughed. "You're completely selfish." He thought living in separate houses sounded good to him too. Everyone needs personal space to help keep the romance alive. Maybe more than one, he thought.

"I might be a little selfish, but not totally." She smiled. "I don't mind sharing myself in some ways."

"*No eres completamente egoísta*?" he asked. "You're not entirely selfish?"

"No," she said. "I like to make love, *me gusta follar.* I like sharing my body...but only with *you*," she added after a beat. "Do I sound selfish?"

"Not to me." He laughed and reached out and stroked the back of her hand with the tip of his finger.

"No. *No es del todo malo*," she said, and turned her hand over, grasped his finger and brought it up to her lips and licked the tip of his finger.

"It's not all bad." She smiled. "I like making love Sunday afternoons. I like being lazy on Sundays."

"Well, I am glad today is Sunday." He laughed. Taking his finger back, he moved closer to her and touched her shoulder. She looked at him and smiled.

"Yes. We have all afternoon." She pushed against him. She reached around and put her hand on the back of his neck, pulled his head down and kissed him. She pulled back, searched his eyes, and in a decisive movement, stood up and faced him.

She unbuttoned the first two of a long line of buttons that ran down the front of her dress. The dress opened to reveal her lacy, black bra, she unfastened two more buttons to revealed her belly, and with the last ones, the dress fell open. She wasn't wearing panties.

He reached out and placed his right hand on the inside of her thigh. The heat of her smooth café con leche colored skin radiated into the palm of his hand.

The tall length of her naked body framed by the opening of the front of the dress was exciting, erotic. Her high heels accentuated the shape of her calves and the muscles of her bare thighs. She reached down and moved his hand higher.

"Touch me," she said, and pushed closer. "Sí, there."

"I love Sunday afternoons," he told her.

"Yes. *Son deliciosos*," she said. "They are delicious." She opened her thighs slightly and moved against his hand.

A small tremor rippled through the muscles of her belly. Her aroma was intoxicating. Her eyes closed, and she pushed harder against his hand.

"*Así*, baby," she whispered. "There!"

21 *Spontaneity*

"I don't think you find me sexy," she said. "That's what I think."

"What?"

"You don't find me sexy," she said, pulling on a pair of thong panties that cost about a hundred times more than they weighed. She turned and stuck her butt out at him. He was sitting on the edge of her bed.

"I don't turn you on." She was examining herself in the mirror and putting lipstick on her sensuous mouth.

"You turn me on plenty." He laughed. "You nearly kill me sometimes. I get so turned on."

"You are making fun." She turned and glanced at him before looking back into the mirror over her dressing table. The table was loaded: bottles of perfume, hairbrushes, nail polish, a jewelry case, and a red bra that she had discarded earlier when she had taken a shower. She rubbed lotion onto her breasts and belly.

"You didn't seem interested this time," she said. She lifted her left breast and touched her still-erect nipple. "Are my breasts too small? Do I need to go to a plastic surgeon? Make them bigger?"

"You are perfect. I love your breasts."

"*No te creo*," she said. "I don't believe you."

"I love your body. You're a beautiful woman," he told her. "*La más hermosa que conozco*, the most beautiful I know."

"No, I'm not." She picked up the red bra. "You don't think I am sexy. I need bigger ones. All men like *tetas grandes*."

"Not all men," he said. "I don't."

"Why don't I turn you on then?"

"You do. Look. I need to anticipate when we are going to make love. I can't be *tan espontáneos*, so spontaneous."

"*Me gusta la espontaneidad*." Her lips pouted in the mirror. "I like spontaneity. I like making love at the spur of the moment. You used to, too."

"Yes, but lately, I need more time to get ready. Viagra does not work in an instant. I need to take it an hour before we make love: Viagra's not spontaneous."

"I'm sexy?" She pinched a nipple and ran her hand down over her flat belly.

"Yes. You're the sexiest woman in Colombia." He got up and stood behind her. He put his arms around her, pulled her back, and kissed the hollow between her shoulder and her neck.

"I love you. You're gorgeous, and you know it. It just helps to plan a definite time to make love. Besides, taking our time *no es del todo malo*, is not all bad, *verdad*, right?"

"You really think I'm sexy?" she asked. She turned in his arms and put her arms around his neck, leaned back, and looked into his eyes. "*Soy sexy de veras*, I'm truly sexy?"

She stepped back, reached down, and touched herself through the thin material of her panties.

"Does it excite you when you see me touch mi cuca like this?"

"Yes, but Viagra needs some time to act." He reached down and put his hand over hers.

"I turn you on when you see me naked. When I do this?"

"Yes. I love making love to you. It's just that I feel a lot of anxiety sometimes, and guessing when to take Viagra puts me under a lot of stress." It was difficult for him to talk about it, embarrassing.

"*Quizás no soy bastante para ti,*" she said. "Maybe I am not enough woman for you."

"You might be too much woman for me." He took his hand away.

"Maybe you should find yourself a younger one." She frowned and turned back to her mirror.

"You are the younger one," he said. He wished he did not need to use Viagra, wasn't getting old. "You don't have any problem being enough woman for me."

"I don't get you excited sometimes," she said.

"Look, here's what I want to do."

"Make love to me?" she said.

"Yes, but first, let's go out."

"I am not dressed to go out."

"Let's get dressed up," he said. "Wear those new pants from Studio F and your new shoes, the patent-leather ones with the real high heels."

"You like the way my ass looks in those black pants, don't you?" she said. "You said they made me look like a model."

"They do. You have the perfect body to wear clothes from Studio F."

"Can we go shopping? I want a new bra and panties."

"Yes, let's go have lunch and, after, go shopping," he said. "We'll go to the crepes place we like."

"*Me amas*?" she asked. "Do you love me?"

"I love you too much," he told her.

"I love you too, baby," she said. "*Te amo con todo mi corazón*."

She turned away and stepped to the closet to pick out clothes to wear to lunch, He popped a 100 mg blue pill into his mouth.

"Me too, con todo mi corazón," he said. "You'll see how much I love you when we get home from lunch and shopping."

22 Shin Kicker Needed

"If you don't have something nice to say, say nothing," my mother, Louise, told my brothers and me often when we were young. My daughter, whom I had asked along to help me follow my mother's advice, and I had a date in Oklahoma City to meet my oldest son for lunch at a new restaurant he'd suggested.

"He is doing well," my ex-wife had told me a couple of weeks before. "He is working out and has his son on every other weekend. They go to the gym, do homework, and enjoy their time together. I am happy for him."

"Maybe he'll turn out to be the son you always wanted, and you the mother," I said.

"You are such an unfeeling bastard," she was happy to tell me. "We never mattered to you."

Whenever I have a chat with my daughter's mother, I definitely need to follow *my* mother's advice and have someone along with me to kick my shins if I do not.

I'd lived in Oklahoma City a couple of years, so I had an idea where we were to meet up for lunch, but I still put the address into my GPS. Naturally, the darn thing led us to industrial park, and I had to backtrack.

In spite of getting lost, we walked into the restaurant on time. My son was waiting for us at the entrance. A tall blond hostess picked up three big menus and let us back to a table not too far from the bar. She seated us along a wall of exposed concrete painted a charcoal that matched the color of her uniform and placed menus in front of each of us. The restaurant was one of those black-and-white decor jobs with exposed ducts and pipes in in the ceiling. Big black-and-white pictures of Oklahoma City from the forties hung on the walls.

My daughter and I sat next to each other on one side of the table, and my son sat opposite on the other side. Probably make it more difficult for her to kick me, but so far, so good, I thought, and smiled at the bar, the pictures, and up at the exposed ducts and pipes under the ceiling.

"This restaurant is owned by the guy who is the president of Chesapeake Energy. He and his partners built the whole shopping complex," my son told us. My daughter was looking over the menu.

"Everything might be out of our budget," she said.

"I think our company, Daddy Hinkle's, can afford it," I told her. "You've got the company making plenty of money."

She didn't kick me. My daughter runs a company that my brothers and I own, and she is doing a great job. We had come to Oklahoma City to meet with one of our distributors, which, unfortunately, would be a victim of the changes taking place in the grocery store business. The smaller distributors just could not compete with bigger companies. Companies adapt, reinvent themselves from time to time, or die, if I remember Darwin's Theory of Evolution correctly.

Since we would be in Oklahoma City on business, I suggested to my daughter she call her brother and invite him to lunch. He agreed to meet us and suggested this restaurant.

I listened to my daughter and my son chatting about work, gardening, my daughter's bees, and kids. She has two and he one—a good-looking boy named Ryder, who I liked but didn't get to see very often.

My first wife and I divorced after nine wonderful, perfect years of marriage. She got custody of our three kids, and a few months later, I got a new six-foot-tall girlfriend. When my son turned fifteen, he came to live with me the summer of 1982. We hung out, played tennis, went out for dinner, water-skied every day that first summer we were together.

We spent a lot of time together the next three years, but I was not paying much attention to a troubled kid. If I could turn the clock back, I'd pay better attention and try to be a father—not a brother and not a buddy, a father.

I found out that our having the same first name could cause a lot of confusion. When we played tennis, I used to talk to myself and still do.

"David, you idiot," I would say aloud all the time after I made a bad shot. Finally, I realized that my son, David, thought I was talking to him. I really did feel like an "idiot."

"Hello, my name is Karen, and I'll be your waitress today," a slender young woman said. "What can I get you all to drink?"

"I'll have iced tea," my son said. My daughter ordered ice water in keeping with her low-budget plan.

"What beers do you have on tap?"

Karen gave me the rundown on the long list of draft beers they had.

"A Foster's, then," I ordered. I read somewhere that an Australian wouldn't touch a Foster's if he was dying of thirst, that they thought Foster's was no better than horse piss—or it could have been another animal. The nice-looking waitress didn't turn up her nose at my choice, so maybe she hadn't read the same article.

"Your new mother," I said, showing my son a picture of my new Colombian wife, who is gorgeous and looks like a model.

"Pretty," he said.

I put the photo away and took a big drink out of my Foster's. It tasted delicious to me. My daughter gave me a hard look but did not kick.

My son ordered a grilled chicken breast with the vegetable medley. My daughter asked if it was possible to order from the child's menu and then decided on a small salad.

"A bacon cheeseburger and seasoned fries," I ordered just for spite after a quick glance at the menu. What I needed was the small salad my daughter had ordered or my son's healthy choice. He had lost weight.

"You look fit," I told him.

"I came here straight from the gym," he said, and went on to tell my daughter that his trainer had introduced him to cross training, how he and my grandson worked out together at the gym and at home too. I didn't ask after the kid's mother. My son and she had never married and didn't live together. I knew her from the time she was with her first husband. She was a hairstylist, had her own shop, and cut my hair when I was in Oklahoma City.

When I heard that my son named my grandson Ryder Davidson, I didn't know what to think. Well, made me think about motorcycles actually, because I had practice riding a big motorcycle in a parking lot on my son's black Harley Davidson Road King. He had loaned it in 2006. I needed to get more experience. Felt as if I were riding on top of a truck at the beginning. He'd had it bored out from 1200 cc's to 1800 cc's and had replaced the normal handlebars with "ape" hangers I had to reach up to grasp.

A year before, I'd gotten a motorcycle endorsement on my driver's license because of a tall, sexy Osage Indian with red Ducati 900. She scared the crap out of me one day when she stopped the thing a few feet behind my back and opened up the throttle full blast. She thought it was funny.

Of course, I fell in love when I turned around and saw her laid out on top of that red machine with a bandana tied around her head to keep her long black hair out of her face, black goggles on her forehead, her skimpy white T-shirt with the sleeves cut off and wearing a super grin on her face. Made me want to mount up and ride for sure.

A two-day motorcycle class learning to ride on a 125 cc single cylinder cycle did not prepare me to test-drive a 1000 cc motorcycle, much less run one that big on the street.

Two weeks of practice in a parking lot on my son's 1800 cc Harley, riding it in downtown Oklahoma City on Sundays and out on the highway a few times, made me more comfortable riding a big bike. Today, every Italian motorcycle I see reminds me of that tall, sexy Osage on her red Ducati.

"Can I get you all anything else?" Karen asked when she came back with our order and set our food on the table.

My son shook his head no, my daughter asked for more water, and I smiled up at Karen and pointed to my empty glass.

"Another delicious Foster's," I told her.

The cheeseburger was huge. They got no idea how to make a hamburger in Bogotá, Colombia, where I live with my beautiful Colombian wife. Burgers in Colombia are too healthy—not greasy enough. They fry up french fries but not the same fries we get in the USA. Better to stick with Colombian food if you ever get to Bogotá. It is great and delicious.

My daughter ate half of her salad, and my son was just cleaning his plate, when Karen came back with the dessert menu.

"The double chocolate cake is my favorite." She smiled.

We refused, and I asked for the check. My son didn't argue. I paid with a company credit card. I overtipped Karen for the great service and not because she was so good looking.

Outside the restaurant, my daughter hugged my son, I shook his hand, and we said our goodbyes. We went out to the parking lot, got into the company's Ford van, and headed to our meeting with the distributor.

"That went well," I told my daughter once we were back on the road, "not one bruise on my shins."

"Well," she said, "you tempted me two or three times." She laughed. "We must do lunch with my brother again. Soon, maybe you two will be mature enough to do it together on your own."

"Maybe," I said.

23 Behind the Writer

"Why do you spend so much time writing? What do you hope to accomplish?" she asked me.

"The why and the purpose don't matter, because I'm not able to stop myself from writing nonsense and drawing pictures," I told her.

"Nonsense sounds like a waste of time," she said.

"You're probably right. Truth is, I blame a guy named Miguel de Unamuno, a Spaniard, for all the paper I waste putting down my vaguely philosophical ideas and other stuff I write that won't matter and is primarily for my own amusement."

"Miguel de who? I never heard of him," she said.

"Miguel de Unamuno. He was a Spanish educator, philosopher, and author, whose essays had considerable influence in early twentieth-century Spain. He died six years before I was born."

"You were born on June 30, 1942."

"Good you remember my birthday. More importantly, I hope you remember the perfect present."

"I know what you want for your birthday; don't worry, but what about what's-his-name?"

"Miguel de Unamuno. He spent more than a minute of his time trying to prove without a doubt that God existed. Miguel wanted to know he had an immortal soul. I mean *know* as in 'able to prove it beyond any doubt.'

"He was an essayist, and I liked his stuff because it was short, and my Spanish was not that good when I was in grad school. I also liked him because he was an opponent of Franco and Fascism. Cost him his job."

"Franco was a king of Spain," she said.

"Not exactly but wanted to be probably. Franco sent a fascist general to drive the old professor at gunpoint from the University of Salamanca on October 12, 1936. 'Death to intelligence! And long live death!' the fascist General Milan-Astray screamed," I said.

"What a horrible man, that general," she said.

"He was. I like what Unamuno said about Franco: 'At times to be silent is to lie. You will win because you have enough brute force. But you will not convince. For to convince you need to persuade. And in order to persuade, you would need what you lack: Reason and Right.' Same could be said about Donald Trump today."

"Sounds to me like that guy was a big influence on you."

"Yes, but the question I asked myself when I read about the event was did his belief in God hold strong when Unamuno lay clutching his chest as his heart exploded two months after he got run out of the university? Was his soul immortal?"

"I don't believe in all that immortal soul business," she said.

"Me neither, but today, when I look in the mirror, I see why Unamuno was so concerned—what he must have seen so many years ago—our weak flesh. I see no doubt in my reflection that we all will physically fall by the wayside. There is no escape. Miguel thought his only hope for immortality to be an immortal soul, but what if there was another way?"

"Another way for what?"

"Forget about the existence of God and an immortal soul. Maybe immortality is achieved through creating works of art, literature, and essays?"

"Believing in God would be easier." She laughed.

"You're right. Most everyone tries to take the lazy man's path to heaven, you ask me, but I have convinced myself that immortality can only be achieved through art, by creating something no matter how small or large that has universal meaning and transcends time. Does it matter? Probably not. I write or paint with the hope that one story or one painting might bring me a faint view of immortality one second before my demise."

"Good luck with that," she said.

"Worked for Unamuno. I think he got his immortality in the end. Do you think Unamuno would be terribly disappointed to know he may have achieved a speck of immortality because a nobody gringo from Oklahoma remembers and admires him for an essay he wrote in 1921?"

"I don't know. But on your next birthday, I am going to show you the true path to heaven and immortality." She laughed. "After, you won't be worried about immortality or about writing timeless transcendental nonsense. You won't have the energy for it."

"Here's to immortality, long live immortality!" I laughed.

24 Something Good

"I don't think you can be creative if you are happy," she told him. He was lying on the bed, watching her apply her mascara. She was putting on eyeliner to accent her almond-shaped eyes.

"Nothing good?"

"No, *nada*, because if you are content, you want to lie around, eat, sleep, and get fat." She turned and looked at him before turning back to her mirror and starting on her lips, then added, "Well, that's not everything you want to do. I know what you think about all the time, Caballero."

"That 'get fat' part doesn't sound good."

"That's because you don't find fat women attractive," she told him. She applied an outline to her lips.

"You like this color of lipstick?" she asked, holding out the lipstick so he could see it.

"Yes, I do," he answered. "A woman who is young is not ugly with a thin layer of baby fat." She gave him a look, raising her eyebrows. She turned back to the mirror and applied color to her lips.

"A thin layer?" she said, and did that thing women do with their lips after they put on lipstick.

"You are young, look great, and have the body of a twenty-five-year-old, and baby fat here and there wouldn't hurt."

"I don't need baby fat anywhere. I am gorgeous, and you know it, and I *do* have the body of a twenty-five-year-old." She laughed.

"You're incredibly exotic. I love your hair and your Colombian eyes."

"I know what you love, and it's not my hair."

"Well...your other parts are exotic too," he said.

"I know what parts you're talking about, and you're right. You Americans think I have extremely exotic parts, and I know you enjoy using them. Me too."

"I'd enjoy using them right now."

"Hey. Be careful, *vaquero*. I have to go."

"Don't go. If you leave me, I won't be happy."

"Create something good. If you're unhappy, you won't lie around the entire day and get fat."

"I don't want to get fat. Being old is enough."

"You're not *that* old. I have to go, *mi amor*."

"Por favor, baby, why don't you stay? Please. We can be creative together."

"If I stay, you'll be too happy."

"You have enough for *el transporte,* cab fare?"

"Yes, as always, you were more than generous," she said.

He walked with her to the door, but before she opened it and stepped outside, he pulled her close.

"Don't go," he told her. "You smell delicious."

"Be unhappy. Create something." She laughed, and then she opened the door, stepped through, shut it behind her, and disappeared.

He went to the kitchen and poured a cup of coffee. He carried his cup of coffee to his office and sat at his computer. Was she right? Was unhappiness the key to creating something good?

"We'll see," he said aloud. He could still smell her perfume and couldn't stop thinking of where she was going or who she would be with next. She was beginning to intrude into his thoughts too much.

"Stop it. You're way too old to be falling in love," he told himself aloud.

25 Thinking

The young man, who asked if he could embrace me, remembered everything; he was cursed with a photographic memory.

"Mostly, he remembered his first encounter," I thought. "I wonder if the priest had been gentle when he molested him the first time."

Why did she come to bed and tell me a divorce was easy, first a lawyer and then a notary?

"Someone's planning," I thought, "not decided yet but has started to make a plan."

A cousin of my grandmother had acre upon acre of black, fertile soil and corn planted row upon row. "Seeds are planted," I thought, "and words. Are thoughts also seeds? Do they grow like weeds and spread?"

Who was it that said thinking is the hardest work that a guy will ever do? "And dangerous," I thought, "especially wondering and thinking about what a lover's planning and going to do."

What are the two most common problems a couple shares after the honeymoon? After they realize what you see is what you get? "Sex is not the first problem," I thought. "Although a guy probably starts thinking about it and missing it after he tries to talk to his new wife about money."

How long after you first think the word does the divorce actually happen? "About six years later than it should," I thought.

26 Pacemaker

I was sitting at my desk in the office the Colombian and I share in our apartment in Bogotá.

"What are you doing?" she said.

"I'm staring."

"What does that mean? Staring?"

"In Spanish it means *mirar fijamente*," I said.

"Stoop it." She laughed. "Do something *divertido*, fun."

"Stupid?" I said.

"Yes, *basta*! Stoop it."

"You mean *stop* it," I laughed, "but you're right. It is stupid. I will *stoop* it and get busy."

"Good. I'm going for a run in the park with the dog," she said. "I'll see you later. Get busy."

The door shut behind them, and silence settled over the apartment. I reached for the cup sitting on the edge of my desk and knocked it over. The startled cat fled the office.

"God damn it," I said aloud.

Fortunately, the cup didn't fall off and break. I used a paper napkin to mop up what little spilled coffee there was on the desk and the floor and went to the kitchen to get refill.

I am getting clumsy in my old age. Lately, I have been stumbling around and dropping things a lot—staring a lot too.

The other day, I got an email from a friend who's in his seventies like me. Ed wrote that he sold his motorhome and motorcycle and bought a red, vintage Corvette. Told me his wife couldn't ride the motorcycle anymore because of her knees. In the Corvette, they could still do road trips. The red Corvette must not be a penis extension for Ed if he's taking his wife along. Probably would be for me.

The runner got back home from the park and walked into the office with the dog following right behind her. She bent down over my shoulder.

"What are you looking at?"

"A map of Uruguay. I'm thinking about taking a road trip."

"Uruguay is a long way from Bogotá, even if you fly," she said. "God knows how far it is from Oklahoma."

"It's about five thousand miles, if you can get there from Oklahoma. Uruguay has a lot of beaches."

"It gets cold in the summer down there," she said. "I am going to take a shower. After, I'll fix us some breakfast."

Maybe I can summer in Colombia and winter in Uruguay, or whichever, since the seasons are reversed here in South America.

"*Tu desayuno para un Rey*," I heard from the dining room. "Your breakfast fit for a king."

I stopped daydreaming about Uruguay.

"Wow. Soft boiled eggs just the way I like them, *arepas con queso*, and hot chocolate. All gringos should be so lucky to live like kings in South America," I said, sitting down at the table.

"*Todos lo fantasean*, they all dream about it." She laughed. "I bet at least seventy percent of old gringos fantasize about getting themselves a young Latina."

"I am *fantaseando* about kiteboarding in Uruguay. I already got a young Latina. Ed sent me an email today."

"Ed and Pat are so nice. For my birthday last year, Pat sent me a bookmarker she'd made, remember?"

"It had a Christian message perfect for an Atheist like you." I laughed.

"I liked it, and it was very nice of her to make it for me. What did Ed have to say?"

"He got a big, expensive surprise for Christmas this year," I said. "He was at the gym, passed out in the locker room. Fell. Hit his head."

"Hit his head?" she said.

"Yeah. Had to go to the hospital. They did all kinds of tests and found out he needed a pacemaker."

"Pacemaker?"

"*Marcapaso* in Spanish. My mother had to have one when she was eighty years old. Her heart had an irregular rhythm, and the pacemaker helped maintain the regular beat of her heart.

"Ed's email made me think about more than taking off your panties…like I do all the time. Started me thinking about what I'm doing with my life. Thinking about not letting life pass me by."

"I like the 'take off your panties' part. I might have to test you to see if you need a pacemaker."

"If I pass out, while you're testing me, I hope I don't hit my head like Ed did." I laughed. "Ed needing a pacemaker was shocking. He´s my age, maybe a year older."

"You're not old."

"If you blushed like I do when I lie, I would know when you were lying."

"You can't see me blush. I have no pink pigments in my skin."

"I love the café con leche color of your skin. You're tan all over. No tan marks."

"I'd have tan marks if I wasn't careful, didn't avoid the sun. I use a lot of sunscreen. I don't want to have wrinkly skin," she said.

"Ed told me they bought an old Corvette so they could still enjoy road trips. Pat's knees won´t let her ride on their motorcycle anymore. They sold it."

"You need to tell her about the vitamins I take. Now, I have no more pain in my hip."

"I will. So, when are you going to test my heart, doctor?"

"Today *is* Sunday." She laughed. "I think we should give your heart a test this afternoon."

27 *Who Was She?*

"Good morning, David," the receptionist said.

"Hello, Elizabeth. I´m early. My appointment is at ten."

"We have one of those new coffee machines. There's an assortment of coffees: Colombian, flavored, and decaf, tea, or hot cocoa. You just pop in the K-Cup pod and push brew. It's great."

"Okay."

I had been living in Colombia, boiling coffee on top of the stove, and pouring it through a cloth strainer. K-Cup coffee pods was pretty high tech for me, but I needed a cup of coffee, so I went over to the coffee maker and picked out a little pod of Colombian from the selection available.

I skipped the directions. Popped in the pod, put a cup under the spout, and selected six ounces. Pushed brew and hoped for the best.

I poured in a couple of little tubs of half-and-half, added a bunch of sugar, and carried my coffee over and sat down and picked up a magazine to read while I waited for my appointment.

A tall woman in a pair of tight jeans cut low at the waist, wearing high-heeled cowboy boots and a leather jacket, came out of the inner office and walked up to the reception desk. Couldn't hear what they said. Elizabeth handed her a card.

"You can go in now," Elizabeth said to me.

I took a last sip of coffee and put down a magazine called *Psychology Today.* The cover announced an article about the good and bad of a modern, long-distance marriage. I could have written the piece from personal experience.

The woman in the tight jeans and I made direct eye contact as we passed. I turned and watched her leave the waiting room.

"Who was the woman who just left?" I asked Elizabeth.

"We're not allowed to give out the names of patients. I'm sorry, David."

"Me too." I opened the door and entered the inner office for my appointment. One way or another I am going to find out who she is…if my therapist doesn't cure me of my obsession…I wonder if I should talk about my newest.

"Good morning, David. How have you been," my therapist greeted. "Take a seat and relax…Let's see…the last time we talked, we were talking about your obsessions with beautiful women…treating women as sex objects…

Worse than Donald Trump, I thought sitting down and relaxing back in an overstuffed chair covered in soft leather across from the therapist, who sat with legs crossed in front of me and slightly to my right.

Good legs. Dancer's legs. I bet she'd be great in…

28 Pieces Torn from Newspapers

"You dreamed you were picking up used syringes?"

"I know. It was crazy. In my dream, I was suited up in one of those protective suits—the blue ones I saw all those people wearing when they were taking care of all those people infected with Ebola over in Africa. But I was walking in a park in Sweden picking up the bloody syringes, not in Africa."

"Usually I don't remember my dreams," she said.

"Me neither, but this time I did. My dream jumped from Sweden to Thailand."

"Thailand?"

"Yesterday, I saw a program on TV, the one where the guy travels all over eating the native dishes—Vietnam, Italy, New York, and yesterday, Thailand. The one with what's-his-name."

"*Anthony Bourdain: No Reservations* on the Travel Chanel."

"Yeah, that's the one. Wait, it wasn't Thailand; it was in the South Seas, French Polynesia, some island. He said he didn't like it much. The place had a funny name, and he said Gaugin, that painter who cut his ear off, didn't like it much either."

"Pape'ete. You're talking about the capital of Tahiti."

"I can't believe it. You know everything. My dream wasn't about food. It was about Tahiti's transsexuals. Rae-Raes is what Bourdain called them. He went to a bar, and after, he had a late night snack with three of them. They looked like women, but were men, I guess. I wouldn't have known if he hadn't said anything; they were so good looking."

"What are you talking about?"

"I don't know. My dream came in flashes of women, men, Rae-Raes. Everybody mixed, some of the women-men had penises, or penises and vaginas; some had no breasts but long nipples; and a few were tall, slender woman except their clitorises were all big like penises. My dream was like a painted collage of pieces torn from newspapers of naked, sexually distorted bodies laid on top of each other with the edges torn."

"Bourdain's show made a big, queer impression." She smiled.

"You think my dream means I'm sexually messed up?"

"I do." She laughed. "Totally."

29 *Self-Interest*

"The president of the United States is so stupid," she said.

"I voted for him twice," I said.

"You probably voted for Bush twice too," she said.

"No, but my brother did." I laughed.

"Senator Robledo of my political party said that Americans don't have friends; they have interest," she said. "You Americans only act out of self-interest."

"I think every county—everyone—does," I said.

"You think I act out of self-interest?" she said.

"We were talking about gringos," I said, "about the president being stupid."

"He is. I thought he would be different. Everyone in Colombia was so happy when he won the first time," she said, "the first black American president."

"I know. Right after the election in 2008, I walked into the coffee shop across the street from our apartment, and the girl behind the counter said, '*Ganamos*, we won.'"

"Now, everyone is *desilusionado*," she said. "Now he's thinking about starting another war. That's all you Americans do. You start wars."

"I see your anti-American sentiment is alive and well. I hoped getting married to an American would have softened you up a bit."

"*No ha sido del todo malo*," she said. "It hasn't been all bad."

"I admit I am disappointed in the president too."

"At least this time, the British Parliament voted against killing a bunch of people in Syria. The prime minister wanted to kiss all the Americans' asses again like always," she said.

"I wouldn't mind kissing the ass of Cristina, the president of Argentina, but I am not attracted to the prime minister or the president of the United States." I laughed.

"I am serious, David," she said. "I hope the American Congress votes down your president's plan to send cruise missiles and kill a bunch of innocents in Syria. He'll probably do it anyway. That's what you gringos do."

"Let's talk about kissing ass some more," I said.

"That's all you gringos think about when you come to Colombia." She laughed. "You gringos think Colombians are sexy."

"Well, I think half of you are." I laughed.

30 Truths

He never was present.

Never thought he took part.

He was always distant, passing through on his way to some other undefined destination.

He was one of the actors: the one who stood a ways back, off to one side, the observer, the character pretending to love a beautiful extra, always in the background, just out of focus.

The closer to the action, the more remote he became.

He carried within a blank, unthinking, unrestricted blackness that overshadowed and blurred everything. His thoughts like barroom brawlers who without a single verbal warning surprised the all-talkers with an unexpected violence.

"What did I do," all demanded as he dragged by the foot or by the scuff of red neck the fools outdoors into graveled back lots.

"What did I do," they begged to know as he blooded their hypocritical mouths and twisted their broken noses out of joint.

"Why," demanded the one-night stands whose calls were not returned.

He feels no remorse.

From the past he knows there is no escape.

He finds it impossible to repent. To what end?

Public confessions are for weak men, for politicians who force empty-faced wives to stand by their sides as they confess publicly their sexual hypocrisy.

His dreams come in streaks like bands of storm clouds.

Memories stalk and haunt him, unwanted guests who have stayed too long.

Before dawn, his fingers play upon a computer's keyboard in a stream of consciousness attempt to exorcise demons. The most inexcusable events of his life are disguised as fiction.

False humor makes light of his darkest truths. Pecking at his keyboard, nouns, verbs, and adjectives all dance to the tune of the most hidden and worst of his history.

He will leave all his confessions hidden in files locked up by complicated passwords. Truths made fiction to an empty confessional frees his soul.

31 *Like Me*

His niece always had a new girlfriend. She was a workaholic, made a very good living from her consulting firm, but her girlfriends were problematic. They were beautiful, but most had emotional problems—baggage, she called it.

He was slicing a prime rib that he had cooked and brought over to his brother's house as his contribution to the birthday celebration when his niece came into the kitchen to get more wine.

"I want a beautiful girlfriend like your newest," he told her.

"You can have her," she said. "She's upstairs pouting in the bathroom."

She twisted a corkscrew down into the top of the wine bottle.

"I know why men hate women," she told him. "They are so needy. They always end up asking, 'Why don't you love me?'"

"We don't hate them, at least not in the beginning." He laughed. "Not until they ask that question."

"Why can't women be more like men?" She laughed and popped the cork out of the wine bottle.

"More like me!" She laughed again.

32 On My Own in Chi-Town

Four years ago, almost fifty years to the day after my father died, I got a royalty check from British Petroleum for $81,288. The check was my part of several years of withheld royalties from the sale of natural gas from wells drilled on the land my father bought during or after World War II.

With winnings from poker games aboard ship when he was in the navy in the South Pacific, my father and his father, Carter Southard, bought up almost seven hundred acres in Southeastern Oklahoma. My two brothers and I, along with my mother, all got a share when he died. When she died, we three brothers divided up her share too.

Yesterday, I got another monthly royalty check from BP for a few hundred dollars, and my younger brother called to say he thought the checks would keep coming and probably get bigger over time, that one day all the cars and trucks would convert over to natural gas. For a second I wanted to be rich, but why? At my age my wish list was very short.

The royalty check reminded me that my father was only forty-five when he died. We buried him on a bright sunny spring day. My mother's ashes and her stone are at the foot of his grave, which is next to the graves of my Oklahoma grandparents.

Half a century ago, 160 miles south of Tulsa, a quarter mile east of the town of Quinton, Oklahoma, my brothers and I, and our mother, stood beside the freshly dug hole in the ground at the Quinton City Cemetery. My grandparents from Illinois, my father's two sisters, and their families stood with us and watched the casket lowered into the grave. The backhoe and two gravediggers in bib overalls waited a short distance away.

From his grave, my father's spirit would have a perfect view of the *Sans Bois Mountain Range* and Tucker's Knob eight miles away. Shaped like a volcano, Tucker's Knob was the highest peak in the state. He'd been born at the foot of that peak. My father's body was a long way from Chicago and Aurora, Illinois, where he had died five days earlier.

We all gathered at my aunt's house in Quinton, Oklahoma, after the burial for a lunch of fried chicken, mashed potatoes, sweet iced tea, and all the other stuff that goes with southern funeral cooking. Her house was on the same street and five blocks north of the First Christian Church, where my father's funeral took place.

The church was a low single-story white-framed building with a steeple planted in the middle of the roof. Inside it smelled of furniture polish. From time to time, guest preachers came, tried to save the few souls that remained in Quinton, and baptized innocent children and any who at the last minute hoped for a reprieve and a chance at heaven.

One of my father's brothers-in-law was a lay preacher. He did the honors at my father's funeral. He did a good job. My cousin Hal sang the hymn *Be Not Afraid*. I didn't remember my father ever stepping inside a church, but it did not matter. His funeral was not for him. It was for all the rest of us.

My mother was a widow at forty-five, with my younger brother, who was five years old. I was nineteen years old and a student at the University of Oklahoma. We did not speak of the future after the funeral. I only thought about getting back to football practice and making the football team. We were in the middle of spring practice. I had dreams of playing in the fall.

After my father's death, my mother sold everything and moved to our ranch in Oklahoma, but I was an uptown guy and couldn't imagine not living in the Chicago area. Oklahoma had a great football team, but what about putting on a suit and taking a girl out to dinner and to the theater or a jazz club, or going to a White Sox baseball game, or the Chicago Bears and Lake Michigan. I was no cowboy from Oklahoma.

After classes let out in May, I packed up and headed north. I had a job for the summer waiting for me in Chicago. At first, I got a room at the Y in downtown Aurora and drove into Chicago to work.

Another college kid, who was working like me for Geneva Construction, was staying at a frat house at Northwestern University in Evanston. Most of the members of the fraternity were gone for the summer, and they had rooms to rent. I went with him one day after work and got a bed there too.

In June, I celebrated my birthday with a tall, blond, sophisticated girl I had met two days earlier. My father lay in a grave 746 miles away, down in Southeastern Oklahoma, and I was on my own in Chicago.

33 Party Time

There were a dozen of us crowded into Jimmy's dorm room and surrounding his bed. It was late afternoon, Saturday, three hours before kickoff. Jimmy opened the fruit jar and poured out the capsules and pills onto the bed.

Jimmy suffered from narcolepsy and required a constant flow of amphetamines in his system to keep him from falling down asleep. His doctors gave him an unlimited supply of rainbow-colored pills, little white ones, red and blue ones, pink ones, and black ones. Some acted immediately, and some were time release. They formed a multicolored circle in the center of Jimmy's bed.

He didn't play on our football team but was the team's medicine man. At least, he was to those of us who were friends with him. My roommate, a tackle named Jackson, was a transfer from Arkansas University. He liked the red and blue time release and the little white ones that would kick in just before the game started if he took it ten minutes before kickoff. He reached in and picked out two red and blue capsules and one of the little white pills. I picked up a big, pink time release.

Timing was the key: take the Dexedrine too early and you would run out of steam in the fourth quarter, take too much or too late and you would be up all night. If a guy timed it right and got the right dose, he would be like a raging bull for the whole game, and afterward, he would be as docile as a little lamb. Of course, none of us ever got our doses exactly right. Most times, we took too much.

Before the game, the coach had us all in the locker room for a pep talk. We were lolling around dressed in our green-and-white uniforms. A team from some Podunk U was down from Kansas. We listened to him drone on and on over the sound of us breathing like freight trains with the amphetamines surging through our veins, all of us itching to hit someone. We had to be careful in the pregame warmup not to get carried away with each other.

Once the game started, and we turned loose upon our opponents, we could hit to our hearts' content. It did not matter much to my roommate whether he hit or got hit. He liked the physical contact. We all did. The whole game nobody ever said much of anything. The play was called, and we fired out. We kept firing out on each play until we scored, or until someone made a mistake and we lost control of the ball.

My roommate's nose was broken on the first play of the game against a team from Kansas by a linebacker. Jackson knocked him on his butt, but he got in that one lick with his forearm. Only lick he got. The linebacker spent the rest of the game sitting on his ass after each play, but my roommate's nose was busted. The trainer stuffed two rolled-up sticks of cotton in his nose to stop him bleeding all over us. The cotton sticks hanging out of his nose made him look like some kind of crazy monster. At half time, I saw him swallow the second blue-and-red capsule.

With the Dexedrine singing in his ears the whole second half, every chance he got, my teammate tried to kill that linebacker who had busted up his nose. After the game, the pink beauty that I had taken was still talking to me when I showered and was getting dressed. Jackson stood in front of a mirror and pushed his nose straight with the heel of the palm of his right hand.

"Mother fucker!" he screamed at the mirror.

"Mother fucker," he repeated, and applied a piece of adhesive tape across the bridge of his nose. His eyes were turning black, and the pain made them water, but the bleeding had stopped, so he did not stuff cotton up his nose.

Jackson and I were the last ones left in the locker room, and we both were still breathing hard when finally dressed and ready to leave. The Dexedrine kept pumping and pumping its magic. Jackson had a date with his girlfriend, who was the daughter of a redneck deputy sheriff. She was a half-breed Cherokee Indian, as tall as we were when she wore heels, and probably tougher than both of us put together.

We all told Jackson her daddy would kill him if he found out what they were doing. We also told him he was a retard for messing around with her, but he didn't care about what anybody thought. I didn't either, if you want to know. We had us a party to go to, and we were going to have a good time. We were going to dance all night long.

The team had rented an old, beat-up farmhouse out in the country for the weekend. We had two or three kegs of beer that medicine-man Jimmy was in charge of setting up on ice. He had the music. A lot of girls would show up to help us celebrate our victory. We would get higher, and the beer would be ice cold.

I was ready to party. Jackson looked beat up, but more than ready. We were mean machines. Look out, here we come. Jackson hit the front of a metal locker on the way out as hard as he could with his fist and then kicked the front of it in for good measure. Jackson's girlfriend was waiting for us outside the locker room.

"Oh, baby. Look at you," she said when she saw Jackson's face. "You are seriously messed up, baby."

He grabbed her and pulled her with him to his red Chevy convertible. He opened the passenger-side door and pushed her in. She looked pissed. He went around and got in behind the wheel. The motor started right up. He tuned the radio to a rock station and turned it up. I stood with my hand on the open passenger door but did not get in.

His girlfriend slid over close to him and put her hand on his thigh. She reached out, twisted the radio's dial, and turned the volume down.

"You need to go to a doctor," she said. "You look fucked up."

"No, I'm all right. I fixed it. The guys have the party set up," he said.

"I'm not going to any more of those parties," she said. "You need to get fixed."

"I am not going to get fixed. We're going to the party. We're going to celebrate."

"I'm not going to watch you and your buds get drunk and stupid. You're all pilled up. You're out of control. I'm not going to be trapped out in the country with you drunk and crazy. You need to get to a doctor."

"Fuck that," he said.

"Well, I don't need this shit," she said, slid over, quickly pushed past me to step out of the car. I slipped into the vacated seat, and she slammed the passenger door shut behind me.

Jackson reached and turned the volume of the radio up as loud it would go, put the car in gear, and stomped the accelerator to the floor. The Chevy roared away from the curb. I turned and looked back at his girlfriend standing at the curb. She raised her hand high in the air and gave us the finger.

Jackson did not care. Pain was drumming and thumping his head, and the red and blues were pumping and fucking the blood in his veins to the beat of the music blasting out of the front of the dash. He rolled down his window and howled out into the cold night as loud as he could, "Fuck Me!"

The Chevy roared down the highway. From my opened window, the night air blew hard against my face.

"Fuck us all!" I screamed into the freezing wind.

Jackson laughed like a crazed hyena.

"Fuck everybody!" Jackson screamed into the night, the Chevy's accelerator pegged to the floor.

34 Passive

"You think that passive aggression is something most couples share in their relationship with one another?" I asked my wife.

"What are you talking about?"

"Well, lots of times a guy'll agree to go along with something his wife wants to do or buy and later resent his decision. Be angry that he was obliged to do whatever it was. Feel coerced and trapped into saying okay."

"Well, 'a guy' don't have to do anything he don't want to," she said.

"I don't believe that's true."

"You don't want to do something, don't do it," she said.

"Well, in the future I won't," I said. "But I was talking hypothetically."

I bet I will say yes the next time she wants to go visit her family and be mad about it the whole time I'm over there, I thought.

"I think a lot of 'guys'll see themselves as victims. They get married, have kids with a woman who gets fat, and then they start thinking they lost out. They think they *was* robbed. You ever feel like you *was* robbed?" she asked me a couple of minutes later.

"No," I said. "Why would I?"

"Well, your businesses have been robbed. One was burned down, you lost money when you went into business with your friend, you and your first wife got a divorce, and I bet a lot of other stuff has happened to you over the years I don't know about," she said. "A lot of guys that all that stuff happened to would feel sorry for themselves."

"Okay. You'd be right about a lot of other guys. They'd be falling all over their sorry selves with their hands out looking for somebody to tell them it wasn't their fault," I said. "Not me."

"So you don't think of yourself as a victim?"

"Look, every time I lost all my crap, I felt lucky to get to start over, to have a clean slate, and tried to put off getting trapped by a bunch of new possessions as long as possible." I laughed. "That's my story and I'm sticking to it."

"So you're not materialistic."

"Hell yes, I am. Maybe more than most, but after a while, the shiny wears off the prettiest things, including women. Of course, it'd be nice if somehow I'm not responsible for losing everything. I'd get to start over with a clear conscience, so to speak," I said.

"I don't know if I believe you."

"Well, look. Take that time when my first wife ran off. Hell, I'd gotten to resenting her, and when she took off, I was free. I was happy when the next one left too," I said. "I like starting over—fresh, so to speak."

"You like starting fresh, do you, so to speak? Like starting over do you?" she said.

"I always like the sound of that word *fresh.*" I laughed. "Fresssh. That word makes my heart sing."

"I might like that word too," she said. "You might have a good idea."

"What do you mean?" I said.

"Starting over. Starting fressssh!" She smiled.

"Hey. Where you going?" I said.

"Fresssh," she repeated. "Word has a nice refressssing sound to it." She laughed. "I like the way it sounds."

"Hey," I said.

"Fressssh." She laughed as she walk away.

35 I Won't Tell

He did not use the elevator down to the street. He walked down the five flights of stairs he found at the end of the hall eight doors down from his hotel room. It was six o'clock in the morning. He'd moved into the hotel the night before and had slept badly.

This would be his first day alone in Cartagena. Yesterday, after their week together in the hotel on the beach, his girlfriend had flown back to Bogotá to go back to work. His new, small hotel was three blocks inland. It had a courtyard shaded by a giant mango tree loaded with fruit.

In search of coffee, he stepped out of the hotel into the bright Caribbean sunlight. He walked down the block, turned the corner, and stopped in shock. In front of a small café, blocking the sidewalk and part of the street, was the most astounding sight. He forgot the coffee.

Some were wearing cocktail dresses, some had on miniskirts, and all were dressed for the evening. All were good looking, but one, a black girl, was tall and exceptionally beautiful. She was standing and chatting next to a woman almost as tall and thin. She had the same *café con leche* skin color as his girlfriend. He heard her say, "*Hasta luego*," to the black girl before she walked over to where he was standing.

"Buenos días. *Eres italiano*? Are you an Italian?"

"No," he said. "*Americano*."

"*Te gustaría tener una cita conmigo?*" she said.

He didn't understand what she'd said in Spanish but wanted to.

"Would you like a coffee? Un café?" he said, and indicated a table just inside the open front of the café. She walked with him into the café, and they sat down at the first table, her face and body silhouetted by the bright sunlight behind her.

"Café con leche?" he asked. She nodded yes.

"Dos," he said to the waiter.

"*Estás ocupado más tarde?* Are you busy later?"

"*Voy a explorer la ciudad.* I'm going to explore the city."

"*Estás al hotel?*" She indicated the hotel next door with her head.

"Yes, sí. *Eres de Cartagena?* Are you from Cartagena?"

"No. *De Montería, Cordoba.* I'm here to work. I make enough in three months to last all year," she said, switching to English.

"I was here with my girlfriend," he said. "She had to go back home to Bogotá yesterday."

"I'll call my mother and tell her I'll be late," she said. "*Sólo doscientos mil pesos* for an hour."

"Your mother?"

"Yes, she cares for my daughter."

The waiter set two large white cups with espresso coffee in the bottom and a small pitcher of hot milk on the table in front of each of them. He placed a bowl of brown sugar in the center of the table and gave each of them a spoon that he set on top of a napkin to the right of the cups.

He watched the pretty woman cross her legs, lean forward, and spoon three teaspoons of sugar into her cup. She poured in the hot, foamy milk until the coffee was the color of her skin, picked up the cup, and took a sip. He fixed up his coffee with sugar but did not add as much hot milk. Took a sip and smiled.

"I needed coffee," he said. "Café con leche. *Muy rico.*"

"I have something more delicious," she said, and took another sip of her coffee.

"You are very beautiful, but my girlfriend..."

Her pink tongue licked the outline of milky foam from her lip.

"*No le diré.*" She smiled. "I won't tell."

36 Full of Promise

The afternoon was hot. Springtime in Oklahoma is windy but a pleasant time of year. Flowers start to bloom, trees bud out, the grass is green, and new nests will soon be full of baby birds. Fall is maybe the best time of year in Oklahoma, Indian summer. Clear blue skies and not windy most of the time. Winter can be cold. The wind cuts, and roads get sometimes covered with ice, but you can get daytime highs in the sixties when the jet stream moves north and the winds come from the south.

It was 1961. Life was full of promise. I was nineteen years old and suited up for my second spring football practice of the day. My football suit still wet from the morning drills and scrimmage. It was the end of August, summer, and hot.

Twelve of us were sweating and suffering through drills with Coach Bobby Ward on a baked practice field at the University of Oklahoma. Every day all the varsity players gathered around the head coach, Bud Wilkinson. He would read out the name of an assistant coach followed by the names of the players who would be with him for the hour of drills before we would gather for the day's practice scrimmage.

After Coach Wilkinson read their names, each group would cheer and run off behind their coach toward a designated section of the practice field for their workout. He always read the names of Coach Ward's group last. There was no need for the names of the last twelve or fourteen of us to be read aloud. We were the only ones left. With our heads bowed, eyes casting about for some way to escape, we knew we were condemned.

"Let's go, girls. Time to play," Coach Bobby Ward said every day. We all followed him at a reluctant jog to a far corner of the practice field to begin our hitting drills by the numbers. No cheering from our small ill-fated bunch as we ran off to hell. Bobby was rumored to have been a 180 pound All-American guard at the University of Michigan, a Pitbull, unforgiving and relentless.

We had been at it for about thirty minutes when I saw out of the corner of my sweat-filled eye one of the trainers approach. After a short conversation, Coach Ward walked over to me, and for the first time, he had a look of something other than a fiery intensity about him. He put his hand on my shoulder pad.

"I am deeply sorry," he said.

I took a deep breath, removed my helmet, and headed over to where my cousin Hal and my brother Michael were waiting. My father had been ill with cancer for a long time.

37 Ewww

"I could be a standup comic provided I had a bunch of hecklers in the audience every night to feed me material that I could make fun of," J. W. told me and my friend Jimmy Stevens. "I'd be better 'n that Leno guy."

Jumbo, as Jimmy liked to be called, had lived in Florida for twenty years. He was Canadian but had had no problem adopting the Florida cracker attitude about gun control—no control, in other words. Although cracker is derogatory in much of the country, for Jumbo and in most of rural Florida, it was a source of pride. J. W. was from South Carolina. He was a real estate developer. Jumbo had a construction company called Big Sky Construction. Mostly, he did remodels.

"You know. I always wanted to be that guy, you know, the one dressed like a bad clown that sits on the bench in a dunk tank on the midway at fairs and calls all the people walking by names so they'll want to buy three throws with a baseball. You know, he makes 'em mad, and they spend five bucks to try to hit the target and dunk his ass in the water—you know, that guy. I could do that job standing on my head."

We were sitting at Jumbo's kitchen table. I had a bottle ice-cold Budweiser sweating and making a puddle on the table in front of me, and Jumbo had a big glass of iced sweet tea with a big sprig of mint sticking out and hanging over the side. J. W. had a beer like me. Jumbo had a raggedy towel laid out on the table and had all the parts of his favorite pistol spread out on it. The smell of gun oil was heavy in the air.

"Sitting on your ass in a dunk tank and screaming names at people would be a perfect job for you," J W said.

"Hey, fatty, put that turkey leg you're gnawing on down." Jumbo laughed. "You know, I could win a prize for being the rudest, most obnoxious guy ever to sit in a dunk tank and get baseballs thrown at him. I would love that job. I would be better than the guy at the state fair last year who got fired and got his dunk tank shut down, there was so many complaints about how rude he was. I'd be better at bating the white trash than him—a lot better."

"You'd be real good at it for sure," I said. My wife told me that no woman would choose to be with Jumbo—or with any of us when we were together, for that matter—because of the "Ewww" factor. She told me to look it up if I wanted to know what she meant. I did, and it meant to excite nausea or loathing, to sicken, to offend the taste or moral sense, repel, to be disgusting, to inspire profound aversion or repugnance, to be excited by something offensive: we three together having fun, in other words.

"Ewww," I said to Jumbo. We all laughed. Jumbo thought I'd used the pronoun *you*.

"Hey, double ugly. Yeah, yeww. Where'd you get that stupid hat and your ugly wife?" Jumbo laughed. "All day long I could antagonize the poor losers and their used-up wives and slow kids. It would be a lot of fun, like shooting fish in a barrel. You know, I bet I'd make a fortune."

"Yeah, you'd be perfect, but it might not turn out to be as much fun as you think it would," J. W. said. "You'd sure be irritating though. Plenty of people would spend money on baseballs to dunk your ass. I bet your skinny ass would be wet from the time you opened up until the midway shut down for the night."

"Only problem is there's a lot of people in the world don't know how to take a joke," Jumbo said. "Especially fat women, or even skinny ones, but I bet their fat, dumb ass husbands would want to throw baseballs and dunk me."

"Here in Florida and in South Carolina, where I'm from, they might decide to throw something else," J. W. said. "Probably in Minnesota too."

"I just might have to defend myself." Jumbo grinned. He had his pistol back together; he spun the cylinder and sighted down the barrel out the window toward a bunch of turkey buzzards roosting in a tree in his backyard.

"KaPow!" He laughed and took a big slug of his iced tea.

J. W. formed a pistol with his hand and sighted down his forefinger out the window at the birds.

"Kapow! Kapow! Kapow!" he said. His imaginary pistol kicked up each time he picked off one of the buzzards. "A man has an obligation to defend himself."

"Ewww." I laughed and drank down a third of my beer.

38 Enough

He gathered up all his clothes, every jacket, all his socks and underwear, T-shirts, his sweatpants, slacks, dress shirts, his favorite pair of jeans, two belts, suspenders, an overcoat, an old ball cap, his tennis shorts, five silk ties, and finally his tuxedo and threw everything into a big commercial-contractor-sized black plastic bag. The bag contained almost every piece of clothing he owned.

Next, he dug out of the bottom of the closet all his shoes and boots and threw them into the plastic bag on top the clothes. He was wearing an old pair of jeans, a black T-shirt, and a pair of brown loafers. A black leather jacket hung on the back of a chair placed before his desk.

He picked up the big plastic bag and carried it out of the room. He had to place the bag on the floor to open the door to the apartment. He picked up the bag, squeezed it through the door, slid it out onto the landing, and pushed the door shut with the heel of his foot.

He hauled the bag down the spiral staircase, down to the communal garage, out to the street, and set it down next to the curb. Too bad I am so big, he thought, all the homeless here in Bogotá are too small to wear any of the shoes and clothes.

He went back up to the apartment. He packed up his laptop in his well-used canvas briefcase. He gathered up his Eagle Creek neck wallet that was beat up but held his passport, and credit cards, and hung it around his neck. He opened the wallet, took out a creased photo of his wife, and placed it face up on the dresser. He grabbed the black leather jacket and shrugged into it.

He was leaving a lot of stuff behind that he once thought was important—tennis rackets, camera tripod, all his artwork framed and hanging on walls all over the apartment, the first bed he had ever bought and probably the last he would ever buy.

He picked up a wad of pesos lying next to the photo and stuffed them in the left front pocket of his jeans. He went into the bathroom and brushed his teeth. He rinsed the toothbrush and put it still wet into the inside breast pocket of the leather jacket. He used the toilet and flushed it. He turned away without looking in the mirror, shut the bathroom light off, got his briefcase, and walked down the hall and out of the apartment for the last time.

Outside on the street, he flagged down the first cab that came by and climbed into the back seat. He watched the third-story apartment disappear as the cab turned onto El Dorado Avenue toward the airport.

"Fuck it," he said aloud to himself.

39 Empathetic

I stopped at what looked like an old-fashioned, working-class bar in a little West Texas town on the way back to Dallas. I sat down at the long, mahogany bar running down the sidewall of the place, and ordered a Budweiser draft beer in a frosted mug from the tall blond woman working behind the bar. She had been very pretty once and still looked good in a sexy but hard way.

It was early afternoon, and as I was her only customer, she asked me where I was from. I introduced myself. One thing led to another, and we somehow started talking about exes. She said her last husband never had a happy day in his life after his first wife ran off. He was an alcoholic, but she hadn't known it until she started living with him full time. The marriage was doomed from the start.

"I should've known better but married him anyway," she said.

"'What the hell is wrong with you?' is what I used to say to my first wife all the time," I said. "The woman was inherently unhappy."

"I bet you asking her, 'What the hell is wrong with you?' didn't help much." She laughed.

"No." I laughed. "I was too young to understand how to deal with her."

"You think you would be more supportive now?"

"No, but at least now I would say, 'I understand how you feel that way, Darling.'" I laughed.

"That is a major improvement," she said.

"Well, in my mind it means the same as 'What the hell is wrong with you?' But it does sound better."

"You want another beer?" She pointed at my empty glass.

"I would. I'm enjoying the company," I said.

"Me too," she said.

"You're a very pretty woman," I said.

"You're just saying that?"

"I wouldn't have said if I didn't think it," I said.

"I got a good idea about what you're thinking." She laughed and set the fresh draft in front of me. "The beer's on the house."

40 Ears

Last week, I saw my friend getting out of his prized 1950 green Cadillac Coupe Deville, and he had his head wrapped up in what looked like a big white turban. I didn't have time to talk to him, and it wasn't until yesterday, almost a week later, I finally got a chance to say hello. He had replaced the turban with an elastic band around his head that covered most of his ears.

He told me that he had had his ears cut off and replaced flat against his head to celebrate his twentieth birthday. He'd always worried that his ears stuck out too far and decided to have them fixed. He went to a local plastic surgeon that performed the operation at a small private hospital.

He said they gave him a local anesthesia, and he spent the entire operation gazing up into the greenest and most beautiful eyes of the doctor's assistant nurse. Her eyes took his mind off the noise the shears made when the doctor was cutting on his ears.

He said he didn't stay in the hospital after the operation because he believed the brochure that described the procedure as quick and easy and as an outpatient operation. However, once he got back to his little apartment, and the anesthesia wore off, the swelling began, and the pain and drumming started for real. He described how he'd lain in his cot and suffered for two days until finally, desperate, he'd removed the bandages and relieved the pressure on his swollen ears.

He said he now had a new and different idea what the words *stoic* and *tough* meant. He took off the ace bandage that he was wearing and showed me the result of all his pain and suffering. His ears were pinned back against the sides of his head.

"You look okay, better, I guess," I said, "but I never noticed your ears sticking out."

"Like jug ears," he said. "They stuck out just like big jug ears."

41 *Just Get Along*

Today, after lunch, I was sitting at my desk thinking about a young woman, a neighbor. I didn´t know her but had seen her earlier this morning. She lived across the street on the second floor—the top floor—in the building directly across from our third-floor apartment. The room we use as an office faced her bedroom window. Our office has a couple of desks, two freestanding bookcases stand against the inside walls, and examples of our artwork—mostly mine—hang on the walls.

The wall facing the street to the north has a large built-in bookcase filled with books. To the right is a large picture window that lets in plenty of light and gives a panoramic view of the corner of Calle 25B and Carrera 40 that is the dividing line between the neighborhoods of Los Recuerdos and Quinta Paredes.

You can see a bakery, a laundry, and some small shops to the left; on the corner is a Domino's Pizza; and across the street to the right is the Colombian's best friend's house. The neighbor's apartment is on the second floor directly across from the window. The neighborhood reminds me of New York: lots of people always about; street venders serving empanadas and fruit cups; lots of bakeries and restaurants and hotels that serve the convention center and the American embassy that are a few blocks away. We don't have to leave our neighborhood for anything. Our apartment is on the Los Recuerdos side of the line and is middle class by Colombian but not by American standards.

Daylight starts in Bogotá at the same time every day. My wife leaves for work just before it starts getting light outside, around five thirty. Today, after she left for work, I went into the kitchen and poured myself another cup of coffee. As I walked back into our dark office carrying my coffee, I looked out through the big picture window at our neighbor's building.

I could see clearly into the second floor bedroom. The overhead light in the room was on, and the vertical shades of the large window that stretched across the entire wall of the bedroom facing the street were open.

A young woman walked into the lighted room. She was naked. I reached for the light switch by my office door, but I didn't flip the light on. I stood in the doorway back from the window. The young, naked woman reached and grabbed an almost-transparent robe and threw it over her shoulders. It did not close and did not cover her large breasts. I stood in the doorway with finger on the light switch, my coffee growing cold in my other hand. Obscured in the shadow of the doorway of my dark office, I looked into that brightly lit bedroom and watched.

The young woman bent over, stepped into a pair of thong panties, and wiggled them up over her hips. She walked over to a dressing table that sat pushed up against the far wall of her room. She stood with her back to the window and applied deodorant under each arm. The short robe rose up, and I could see her thong panties, the shape of her ass. Her breasts were visible in the mirror on the wall above the dressing table. She picked up a brush and began brushing her hair.

Finally, I got a grip on myself. I walked to our dark office window to close the curtain, but I wanted to watch her finish getting dressed. She was tall, and young, but was not exceptionally pretty, but still, I wanted to watch. I closed the curtain.

At one thirty in the afternoon, my wife got home from work. She was excited.

"One of my poems got published in this magazine," she said.

She handed me a copy of a magazine published by the *Comisión de Asuntos de la Mujer*—a magazine dedicated to women´s rights and feminism. On the back cover was her poem, *Mis Mares*, My Seas. She sat down at her desk by the door of the office and turned on her laptop.

As in most of her poetry, this poem had a couple of references to Greek mythology. The first line was "*La nave Argos*," the ship *Argos*—the boat built by Argos, baptized with his name, and used by Jason in his search for the golden fleece. Jason and his crew called themselves the Argonauts after the boat, if I recalled correctly from my class of Western Civilization 101.

In the second verse, she mentioned the Ocean of Tetis, which in antiquity was the name of the Mediterranean according to the Colombiana. I had no idea.

Her poem was wonderful, and, of course, written in Spanish. She wrote of the immense seas she carried inside herself. How, with the launching of the ship *Argos* in ancient times, her waters were splashed high in tiny misty drops and dispersed by the wind to fall in torrential rains and run back to the sea in the rushing floods of modern times.

I loved her poem. Her poetry was so much better than mine—always written with such passion and with meaning and references gleaned from philosophy and mythology. Mine was mostly trivial and egocentric and mostly had to do with leaving, mostly being told to go and to get out.

"One of my *compañeros* said my poem made him think of semen running though my hair and over my shoulders," she said, after she saw I had read the poem.

"I, of course, laughed at his crude joke and went along with it." She added a mockingly fake laugh and made a face to show me how she had reacted to her fellow teacher's comment.

"I don't know which was worse," I said, "your companion for his thoughtless and classless comment or you letting him get away with his crude and tasteless joke about your exquisite poem."

"You can't say anything bad to *tus lectores*, your readers," she said. "You can't tell them they are stupid, no matter what they say about your work."

"I can," I said, "and probably will."

"You have to respect what they say, David."

"No, I don't," I told her. "Get back, dog, you're getting my pants dirty is what I would have told the idiot, if he had made his stupid comment to me.

"*Bájate perro, me estás ensuciando los pantalones*," I repeated in Spanish, to make sure she understood what I had said.

"You won't have many readers for your book if you have that attitude," she told me, and then, she stood up and went to the door. "Nobody will want to read your book if you call your readers dogs and tell them to get down because you think they're getting your pants dirty."

"At least the ones that *do* read the thing won't be complete idiots like your *compañero*," I mumbled aloud to myself.

She left the room, telling me over her shoulder, "I don´t think your poetry or stories will make your friends think of semen running through *your* hair and over *your* shoulders."

"That's not funny," I called after her.

I heard her laughing in the kitchen. Why I was so offended by the guy's stupid and crude remark about her poem I didn't know. Maybe I was jealous. Maybe it bothered me that he would think about his semen in her hair. Mostly, I was irritated that she would put up with the fool, or maybe I wanted her to...I wasn't sure what I wanted her to do.

Did I see some of her companion's crudeness in my own actions? I didn't know why my reaction was so hard—so negative. Did I see my finger still on that light switch by my office door, and me standing there in that dark doorway looking across the street into that brightly lit bedroom? Did I want to see my semen running in her hair—running in whose hair?

"Here," she said, coming back into the office and handing me a plate with a slice of chocolate cake. "Eat some of this. It'll make you forget about semen." She laughed.

"Maybe," I told her. "My brother Michael told me one time that I should not be allowed to deal with the general public. He thought my attitude was too critical and hard. Like you, he probably thought everyone should get along—not call people fools.

"He was right," she said, and sat back down at her desk and turned to her computer.

Well, maybe, but then, maybe not, I thought.

I read the poem again. It was superb. You should have looked the fool up and down with that famous, hard look you reserve for me when I say stupid things you don't like, I thought. You're a very good poet and writer, and you need not suffer fools.

The poem was beautiful just like its author—both a lot more beautiful than our young neighbor across the street. At least, I didn't remember her as beautiful.

I might have to check again tomorrow morning, after my truly beautiful, talented poet leaves for work at five thirty, just to make sure, I thought.

I sat at my desk looking down at the poem and thought about semen and poetry filled with Greek mythology. I thought of young, naked women brushing their hair in front of mirrors and old men standing in the dark watching. I looked out the window of the office. It was a beautiful day in Bogotá. The sun was shining.

What the hell was wrong with me? Do you automatically become a dirty old man when you reach your seventies?

I looked out the window again at the building across the street. The blinds behind the window of the young woman's bedroom across the way were shut tight.

42 Obligations

Elizabeth stepped from the shower and used a rough towel to dry her back and shoulders, legs, feet, and between her toes and to dry and style her short hair. She brushed her teeth, palmed water with a faint smell of the sailboat's tank into her mouth, and spat the taste of toothpaste and stale water into a small oval sink.

Two tan fingers combed long, black pubic hair, caressed, pushed inside, and withdrew. A round mirror pegged on the bulkhead reflected green eyes too old for her young freckled face. She switched off the dome light and stepped naked into the shared forward cabin.

Her twin brother reclined on the starboard bunk. A thin line of moonlight entered a porthole and ran in a straight, white line across his naked belly. She stroked his cheek. He grasped her hand and kissed the palm.

"I have to convince the captain to let us stay aboard. He's our only chance."

She bent and kissed his mouth.

"I won't be long."

She slipped out and walked through the soft light of the boat's main cabin, her thin, bare feet silent on teak and holly veneer. Fingertips pushed open the aft cabin door.

Her dark shape floated to the edge of the bunk, and a hand slipped under the sheet, caressed his thigh, moved higher, felt him harden. Mouth warm and moist replaced her fingers.

Arms embraced shoulders, small breast pressed against muscled chest, hips lifted, and legs straddled with knees wide. She plunged upon a rod of hot indigo heat. Heartbeats, convulsion, a stifled moan.

Her mouth found him yet erect. Merciless, ruthless fingers explored deep; hungry lips and tongue consumed her, wet and swollen. Enflamed, back arched, fingers crammed into mouth, racked with exquisite pain and pleasure, blood and tears, and at last.

"Daddy!"

The door of the captain's cabin clicked shut behind her. Supported against the teak of the passageway, she leaned back and clawed a finger deep inside. Eyes closed, she pinched and punished a nipple between forefinger and thumb as hard as she could. I'm sorry Mommy. Don't spank me…

"Did the captain agree to let us stay?"

"Yes, he will want us to stay." Elizabeth pushed up onto the bunk opposite her twin's. Covering herself with a worn cotton sheet, she turned toward the outer hull and laid her head on a thin pillow smelling faintly of mildew.

43 Daybreak

Gray ambient light from the two portholes over the gimbaled propane range brought morning to the galley. A ring of blue flame heated a large cast-aluminum espresso coffee maker. The aroma of coffee drifted through the boat. He sat at the chart table with his laptop.

"That coffee smells delicious."

Elizabeth in shorts and a white cotton long-sleeved shirt, barefooted, crossed to the chart table and bent over his shoulder to look at the chart. The Gulf Coast of Florida glowed on the screen, her breath warm on his neck.

Her perfume…no it's not the same. Nothing's the same. Stop it.

"Coffee mugs above the sink. A can of condensed milk is open in the fridge. Café con leche," he managed. Fingers caressed his shoulder.

"Thanks for…making coffee," she said. She straightened, stepped back, and moved to get down the cups. "And for last night."

"About last night…"

"Morn," Jason mumbled as he came into the main cabin and flopped down on the red cushions of the settee running along the starboard side of the boat.

"He almost talked." Elizabeth laughed, seeing the look on the captain's face. She turned her face away and bent to get the milk out of the fridge. "Must've had a good night."

The captain cleared his throat. "Due south it's almost two days to Key West, if we have good wind from the east." His fingertip traced the route on the screen of his laptop. "The forecast calls for twelve to fourteen knots."

She turned off the burner, wrapped a dishcloth around the handle, and picked up the pot. She looked at Jason.

He shrugged his shoulders and moved to sit at the table in front of one of the large white porcelain mugs.

"He said his one word for the day." She poured coffee into the three mugs. "Scoot around the table, Jason, so the captain can sit beside us.

She sat and pushed a hip against Jason's thigh. "Come join us."

The captain turned his laptop off and moved to the table. He slid in next to Elizabeth, and she placed her left hand on his thigh.

"My two men." Elizabeth picked up her coffee mug, took a sip, and smiled. "So delicious."

Jason's hand stroked Elizabeth's thigh hidden under the table. He watched the captain add the thick, sweet condensed milk to his coffee, stir, and lift the mug to his lips. A thin smile played and disappeared. He reached for the can of condensed milk.

We'll soon find out how delicious. Yes.

"Captain, do we *have* to leave today?" Elizabeth looked at Jason and took another sip of the strong, black coffee.

"I thought you wanted to head south."

"Yes." She squeezed his leg and moved her hand higher. "We don't have to hurry, do we? We could spend the day relaxing and getting to know each other."

The captain glanced at Jason, who stared back without blinking.

"Getting to know each other?"

"Yes, the three of us." Elizabeth brushed her fingers across his crotch. "Jason has special talents."

"Talents?"

"Yes, he's trained...an expert. We both are." She smiled. "You'll see," she said, and touched him through his shorts.

"I don't know. Some fantasies may be left...well, fantasies," the captain stammered.

"Some fantasies are worth trying, Captain. Let's have breakfast. After, we see about your fantasies. How do you like your eggs?"

Jason smiled openly for the first time.

44 The Last Tryout

"You think I am beautiful?"
"I think you are very, very beautiful."
"You only wanted me because I am beautiful?"
"I wanted to be with a beautiful woman, yes."
"I only wanted to fail with a beautiful woman."
"You´re not failing; so far you've been wonderful."
"Well, then I may still have a chance to fail."

"No, I don't think you old; you are perfect."
"That's a possibility I had not considered."
"Your ad said, 'Tryouts at two p.m. daily.'"
"Yes, I like to begin all tryouts early."
"What exactly is the part?" she said.
"A tryout to see if you were put on earth for me."
"A tryout to see if I´m God´s gift to you?"
"Yes, I have been looking my whole life."
"You have been waiting just for me all your life?"
"No, I have not been waiting, I've been looking."
"There have been others. I am not the first?"
"I've held tryouts; I've been looking a long time."
"You've held lots of tryouts for a long time?"
"Yes, many, and it has been a very long time."
"All this has just been a tryout?" she said.
"No, not just a tryout. My last tryout."
"This is the last one?" she said.
"Yes, the last one. I don´t need to hold any more."
"No?"
"No, there will not be any more tryouts."
"I´m the most beautiful?" she said.
"No."
"Other tryouts were more beautiful than me?" she said.
"Yes."
"But, I got the part?"
"Yes, you did."
"But others were more beautiful than I?"
"Yes, but you are more than the most beautiful."
"You are much, much more!"
"I am the best?"
"You are the last."

45 Don't Cost Nothing to Look

He arrived late. He always did on Saturdays. His place was two miles off the highway and fifteen miles from the nearest town—hidden if you didn't know how to find it. The joint was rocking. The dance floor was full of cowboys in ball caps and women too fat to be in the tight clothes they wore.

A fragment of a song from the sixties warping its way around on the jukebox took him back, and for a second, the music transported him to another time—another life. He was back in Chicago, dressed in a bespoke set of clothes, in a jazz club sipping Teachers on the rocks with a lemon twist, and in love without knowing what was down the road.

Then, his vision cleared, and the real world crashed back. Walls and ceiling painted charcoal black with thousands of sparkles reflecting neon red closed in on him.

The music was loud enough to rattle glassware behind the bar. The jukebox pounding out music alternating between rock and roll and despairing country and western songs which reminded everyone, especially him, of love lost and drowned in a thousand shot glasses filled to the brim with bonded whiskey and thrown back and gulped down to ease the guilt or pain of betrayal.

A great percentage of the men who were presently drunk or on their way to getting drunk and filled his bar tonight had been away one time or another. They were loaded down with a lifetime of petty grievances they regularly hurled against each other and at the world in general. He was aware of the nature of the people to whom he dealt out seven-ounce pony glasses filled with ice and whiskey, vodka, rum, and gin with mixers of Coke, 7-Up, Tang, water, and most often, nothing.

All his customers assumed he was on equal footing with them. Now, after proving himself worthy of their respect and tough enough, he was accepted.

He arbitrated their squabbles and most times kept a lid on the pot he stirred every night. He heard them talk as though being away was a form of vacation. They never used the word *prison* when they talked about their time in state prison over in String Town. Perhaps being away *was* a vacation from the torment of daily life on the outside. He dreaded when somehow a normal citizen found his bar. He had to babysit them and make sure none of his regulars acted out (or worse) while the tourists were in the place.

He took a barstool at the end of the long bar that ran the length of the west end of the room. Van, his bartender, put a light scotch and water in front of him. It was one o'clock in the morning. His bar would not close until the last customer left. He didn't have a set closing time. Why would he? The bar had no license, and the nearest law was forty miles away. He was the law in the world he had created not in the seven days as the Lord had done but in twenty-three days after his first bar was burned to the ground by a deputy sheriff. The price he'd paid for too much success and not using the vending-equipment company whose owner was financing the sheriff in the backwoods of Latimer County, Oklahoma. His new bar had convinced everyone he was here to stay.

"Your brother called," Van said. "He's driving down from Tulsa tomorrow. He said he'd be here about noon."

His brother was in the business too but was closer to civilization, licensed, and had to close at two. One time, after closing his own bar, he drove down and arrived at four o'clock in the morning. With music blasting, full of methed-up wide-awake drunks, and everyone reeling and screaming at each other to be heard over the thunder of the music, his brother told him that his bar looked like the most dangerous place in the world.

The building built of cinder block had no windows. Daylight was barred entry. The dominating theme was black and the lighting indirect and red. Two oblong lights over a pair of pool tables were the only brightness allowed and only extended to the edges of the green felt.

The neon of the jukebox made a rainbow glow in the middle of one wall. After his divorce, he had made the place home to a constant madness to which all who dared to enter were invited and from which he could not claim to be immune.

He saw her walk in at two o'clock. She came in behind a man and woman. She paused as she stepped inside the door. She stretched a hand out as if to feel her way through the haze of cigarette smoke set on fire by the red indirect fluorescence of the lighting. Her eyes adjusted, and unsure what to believe, she looked over the crowd.

He watched her follow her two companions to a table in the far corner by the dance floor. He motioned a waitress over and told her he wanted to buy their drinks.

He never messed with women who came into his bar. Most were not beautiful, and he was not attracted to them for many reasons, mostly because the women were a draw for his male customers. He worked his way toward her table, shaking hands, greeting customers, and chatting a second or two with drunks who believed they were his best friends.

He didn't take his eyes off of her. Was she an extraterrestrial from another planet? Or maybe a hundred-year flood that only happened once in a lifetime. Her entrance charged the air with static electricity.

Jet-black hair, teased high, fell back past her shoulders in a blue-black reflection of light. Later, in the dawning light, up close, he'd see her eyes were indigo blue. Her beauty and how tall she was set her apart. For him it was as if a spotlight cut her out and dimmed all the other scruffy, dilapidated humans who populated his bar. She was a beacon at the end of a long, lonely tunnel, a lighthouse that signaled danger and served as a beacon to safe harbor.

She sat with her back to the wall, one long leg crossed over another. She had small, firm breasts, and unwisely in this place, her nipples were visible under her sheer sleeveless black silk blouse. She did not shave under her arms, which was a surprising turn on for him. He stood at her table.

The white skin of her face and arms smoldered in the light of the red fluorescent eight-foot-long bulbs hidden behind cornice boards he had installed over squares of black mirror tiles glued to plywood and hung around the walls of the bar in eight-foot by four-foot panels. Some said the effect of the lighting excited demented passions. They were probably right. He did not care. Demented passions were fine with him. He was the leader of the uncontrolled pack.

"Don't cost to look, cowboy," she said when she saw how intensely he stared at her. "Touching might be another story."

He felt heat rise up in his throat. He was a freshman in high school again aching to take out the most beautiful senior-class girl. He extended a hand toward the civilian she had come in with, John or Jonathon. He did not remember. The man reached out and shook his hand like an old friend proud that he had taken time to come over to their table.

"My wife," he said, and motioned toward a small, dark woman on his left. He waved in the direction of the reason he had come to their table. "And this is my cousin. He bent down close to her and breathed in the perfume of her skin and hair. Over the blast of music, he told her he was delighted to meet her.

"I bet every man you meet wants to touch you."

"My husband would not like it." She smiled up at him. "He's possessive."

"I don't blame him." He smiled and introduced himself.

"Sandra Lighthorse," she said. "I was joking about that 'don't cost to look' business."

"I hope not." He laughed. "I'm happy you are here."

The waitress came and set their drinks on the table.

"Let me get the drinks," he said, waving away the man's money. He slid a twenty-dollar bill onto the girl's drink tray.

"May I join you for a moment?"

He sat down next to her without waiting for an answer.

"Where's your possessive husband?" he said.

"He's fighting with his unit in Afghanistan. He's a marine. This is his second deployment there. He was in Iraq before that. He's been gone off and on for three years."

"He sounds dangerous," he said, dismissing the man from his mind. "How did you end up lost down here in Latimer County?"

"My mother lives in Wilburton. My cousin too," she said. "I was in a car accident in Minneapolis, and I'm here recuperating. Nothing too serious. My cousin offered to show me the sights of Wilburton. It took about two minutes, and we decided to come out here."

"I'm glad your cousin brought you. No one ever comes to my bar unless a customer brings them the first time. I don't get many innocent civilians."

"I hope I'm not too innocent for your place."

"I'll have to make certain you don't get into trouble."

He had to leave them but managed to work his way back several times to her table. He watched her dance. She was taller than most of her partners. She did not invite any to sit down at her table.

He invited Sandra and her cousins to go to breakfast with him after the bar closed. She thanked him but declined. Later he saw her sitting alone.

"My cousins had to leave. You still want to take me to breakfast. I could use a ride back to town," she said.

"Why don't you sit at the bar while we shut the place down?" he invited her.

Once all the waitresses and customers were out the door, Van counted the take and paid himself.

"I'm out of here," he said, and laid the money bag on top of the bar. "You two don't anything I wouldn't do."

"You want a drink for the road?" he asked her. She shook her head no. He went around to the back of the bar and turned off all the lights, leaving a small cone of white light on over the bar so they could see their way out.

She was sitting just outside the edge of the light. One white hand was visible on top the bar. The black of the room surrounded and pressed in on them. He moved from behind the bar and walked to her. He sat down next to her with his back turned to the quiet, empty darkness. "Are you hungry?"

"No."

He pushed his hand into the light and with a tip of his finger touched the nail of her index finger. The nail was painted bloodred and looked long and sharp enough to cut into his heart. She leaned her face into the light.

"Do you want me to take you back to town?"

"No," she said. "I don't think I do."

46 No

"A guy, some expert, said old men mostly remember things that happened to them when they were eighteen to thirty years old, maybe even younger," I said.

"An expert said?" she said.

"Yeah, but I don't remember what kind, but it got me to examining my memories to see if it was true."

"You remember what happened in bed this morning, I bet, and you're not eighteen or thirty years old."

"Well, my short term memory is still intact," I said, "but I am talking about when a guy is thinking about stuff that happened—a memory of an event, say, that happened to him pops up sort of unconsciously. Suddenly he's back in high school or college or somewhere like that."

"I bet mostly you remember some girl." She laughed.

"You might be right. Like just now the word girl brought back a memory of a girl in high school who told me no."

"I bet that didn't happen too often," she said.

"All the time," I said, "but this was the first time, and she didn't offer any reasons or excuses after she told me no. I asked her out to go to a movie, and she said no, nothing more, only no. Didn't say I have to study, I have plans, I don't date dorks, nothing. She just said no. I remember feeling stunned. I wanted to know why not, but she just turned and walked off."

"I'll start doing that. I like it. Just say no." She laughed.

"Most people find it hard to just say no, me too. Hey, it's almost noon. I am hungry. Do you want to go out to lunch? I have been thinking about going back to that Thai place again. We'll make it a date," I said.

"No," she said.

47 *Muriendo de Hambre*

Al verte tan exótica y tan deliciosa,
No debo sentirme muriendo de ganas?
Al verte los ojos tuyos llenos de fuego.
No debo sentirme quemado por tus llamas?
Al mirarte tu piel color café con leche,
No debo querer beberte por tu sabor?
Al pensar en mi mujer tan hermosa,
Imposible no querer hacerte el amor?

—Bogotá, June 1, 2011

Dying of Hunger

Seeing you so exotic and delicious,
Shouldn't I be overcome with desire?
Seeing your eyes so full of fire,
Shouldn't your flames burn me?
Upon looking at your café con leche skin,
Shouldn't I thirst to drink all of you?
Thinking only of my beautiful woman,
Impossible not to want to make love?

48 What Do You Want?

He had carefully showered, shaved, and dressed in a loose pair of slacks and a shirt partially unbuttoned to reveal his chest. He was barefooted.

She had chosen the snakeskin high-heeled boots from Italy, and the black miniskirt she wore accentuated the café con leche color of the bare skin of her thighs. A loose silk blouse barely hid her high breast, and her dark-brown nipples were clearly visible. Her makeup was light and subtle, but she had accented her almond-shaped eyes—those Colombian eyes that always fascinated him.

She pressed up against him, reached down, and touched him. He had become excited just watching her move toward him. He could almost taste her.

"*Eres tan hermosa*," he whispered. "You are so beautiful. I am filled with *deseo*."

He was her latest, an American, *mi Viejo*, her old man, she kidded him. She was not the first but *la última*, his last woman, he told her, and his first true love.

She pressed him back against the wall, slid her hand down inside his pants, and touched him. With her other hand, she pulled his head down and kissed him. Her exotic, ripe, and fruity perfume whetted his appetite for more than just a taste of her. He knew how delicious and wet she would be. She looked at him with her exotic eyes. When do they learn to do that, he asked himself.

"*Te amo los ojos tuyos*," he told her, and kissed her again. "I love your eyes."

She pulled back and gave him her eyes again.

"*Yo sé lo que amas.*" She smiled. "I know what you love."

Her hand moved inside his pants and squeezed him. She felt him grow larger. Her dark nipples were hard against the thin fabric of her blouse.

"I am very excited. *Te amo demasiado.*" He pulled her close. "I love you too much."

"*Ya te creo.*" She laughed. Her fingers stroked him. He had become very hard. "I believe you."

She kissed him again and moved her free hand between her own legs. She spread her legs more, and her skirt slid up her thighs. Her eyes became glassy as she touched herself, and her lips parted. He reached down and touched her hand moving between her legs, felt her increase the rhythm and pressure of her finger on her clitoris as she masturbated them both.

In her high-heeled boots, she was as tall as he was. She spread her legs, and he touched her. She was very wet.

"*Qué quieres,* Vaquero?" She laughed and pushed against him. "What do you want, Cowboy? Qué quieres?" She pushed hard against him again.

"*Tú sabes*," he whispered. "You know."

49 Baby

She touched his erection through the silk material of his boxers instead of a good-morning kiss. She ran a finger down his "piss hard," as an ex-girlfriend described the early morning erection a man often wakes up with and that disappears as soon as he pees.

"Hold that thought," he told her. "I'll be right back."

He shook the last drop out into the bowl, flushed, gargled with Listerine, washed his mouth out with tap water, and returned to the kitchen, his erection gone, but his penis still extended. The girlfriend was right.

"Coffee?" She pointed to the coffee maker and handed him a cup. "Hot milk's on the stove."

He set the cup down, moved behind her, and embraced her. His hand slipped into the front of her long nightgown and cupped a breast. He kissed the back of her neck. Thumb and finger caressed a nipple.

"Stop that." She turned in his arms. Her nightgown shifted and exposed her breast. She reached behind his neck and pulled his mouth down to the nipple.

"I mean it." She laughed and slid a hand down into the front of his shorts, wrapped her fingers around his penis, and masturbated him until his penis was fully erect again.

Hands under her arms, he hoisted her up onto the counter. Her hand guided him between her engorged lips. She wrapped her legs around his back and pulled him close.

"*Quiero todo*, I want all of you." She bit down on his shoulder

50 Unlucky Mix-Up

Yesterday's *Tulsa World Online Edition* published a short article describing how a small, shy, ugly man was torn to shreds at a conference held at a local Holiday Inn Express. Apparently, a group of women's righters expecting to hear speakers dealing with sexual and domestic abuse were admitted to a conference dealing with the value of legalized prostitution.

The report was sketchy and did not have many details. The *Tulsa World* promised to publish a full report of the tragedy as soon as the Tulsa Police released the 911 tapes and the full homicide report. The police are also looking at the hotel's security tapes and reviewing the guest list of the hotel, but so far no arrests have been made.

The *Tulsa World* obtained the following transcript of Mr. Underman's opening speech, which he gave at the conference. It is believed that his speech was responsible for the riot and mindless violence:

Good afternoon, my name is Teddy Underman. I want to thank everyone here at the conference today for coming. Let me say that I know my topic, 'Are Hookers Better than Wives?' is controversial, but let me start the conference with the reason's I believe, for a guy like me, hookers are better.

I have had such bad luck with relationships with women all my life.

Instead of trying to date regular, decent, moral women, I decided that it is preferable to pay a hooker for sex and be done with it.

I am a perfect fit for someone who needs to use a hooker. I am ugly, shy, and have no personality. I have had bad luck finding the type of woman I want, and when it comes to the looks department, on a scale of one to ten, I am a one. I am thirty-one years old and still a virgin. I believe it would be a lot easier to go to a hooker rather than wait for another twenty years to meet a nice woman the normal way and get married so I could have sex whenever I want.

I do not believe a hooker would judge a man based on looks, or at least they would be kind enough to lie and not tell a guy how ugly he is to his face. A hooker will do anything a guy wants, for a fee, of course. Hookers do not care about the size of a guy's business either.

A guy can have sex with a ten on the physical-looks scale, even if he is a one, as long as he has enough money. If he goes to a hooker in a legal brothel, where the girls get a regular checkup, they will probably be cleaner than the average woman I will never have sex with probably. The most important thing for me is that hookers are available and willing.

Because they are professionals, hookers are probably better at sex than normal women are, especially if the woman is religious. Having sex with a hooker is probably the only and best option for me, if I don't count fat and ugly chicks, and I am sure hookers are cheaper than a wife, because in the long run, in the inevitable divorce, courts always end up siding with the wife, and a poor bastard like me ends up being financially raped.

I know I am not the only guy that feels this way, and I am sure everyone in the audience agrees that hookers are better than a wife is.

I will now take comments and questions from the floor.

Below are some examples of comments from *Tulsa World*'s readers:

- What a sad ending to a man with the right idea. My suggestion is to find a nice hooker who is not that pretty and convince her to be your girlfriend. Tell her it doesn't matter that she's a hooker and you love her for who she really is.

- I feel so sorry for the poor fool. He should have quit saying all those things about himself. Who said being shy is unattractive? And there is no such thing as an ugly human. Just because you think you are ugly, not everyone else thinks that you are. It sounded like Teddy had personality; at least his question did. Can a hooker give you love?

- You can't kill a good idea; however, you have to be careful not to be giving your girlfriend or wife crabs, syphilis, and gonorrhea. Most of the time, they usually get pissed.

- I wish I had been at that conference. Check places like Craigslist "w4m" or "casual encounter, w4m, mw4m" and find what they call a friend with benefits or a couple looking for a male partner. It is a lot safer, and everyone can use a new friend. I would have told Teddy before it was too late.

- Teddy was simply telling the truth. He didn't deserve to be shredded. I think he did a real good job of describing what most men's needs are. While some men really need emotional attachment, if you don't, then go get them unlicensed sex therapists.

- He did not deserve what he got, but I read self-contempt in his words; if you do not respect yourself, no one else will do. As for his question, depends on what you are looking for: a sex mate or a soul mate?

- Only losers take the "easy" way out. A lot of those guys wind up with diseases, or they wind up alone and lonely. It might sound good, in theory, but truthfully, you should not try it. It's better that he was shredded.

- He was an idiot. He admitted he was no kind of catch whatsoever, but he was very shallow about looks. What a 100 percent d-bag. I never thought I'd answer this way, but yeah, hookers would have been best for you, Teddy. You reap what you sow.

- What a sad excuse for a "man," who did not deserve a wife or a decent girlfriend. He deserved a hooker, and now he is where he should be.

- For you, hookers were better because you had no personality and nothing special about you—so, yes, for you, BUT you would have had a pretty sad life. I am not sorry! I wish I had been there to beat on you too!

- Jesus had one; he saved her from being stoned to death. I don't know if he ever did anything with her or not, but he did like her. Maybe you can ask him, Teddy, if you are not in the other place.

- I bet even hookers wouldn't touch you, you loser. I bet you died a virgin, Teddy boy. At least you didn't get a nice STD as a parting gift.

- "Those girls are probably cleaner than some girls who have had serial monogamy." That offended me. The only man that I have been with is my husband, and you said that hookers are cleaner? Was this a real question? Teddy, you had some negative views of women. Bad luck with relationships meant that there was something going on with you. Now, you can't keep blaming all of the women you meet. There is something that men have to change about themselves. Maybe most of those women were in the wrong too, or mainly in the wrong, but relationships (good and bad) are designed to help us grow. If you can't grow from them, of course you won't be happy. Probably best that you are in heaven or wherever.

- Poor little guy had a different set of expectations, and now I hope he is in a better and different relationship—one with God. Here's what I know: a prostitute will provide attention and sex, for a set period of time, for a set fee, after that, you're expected to pay for another hour, or get out. It is a financial transaction, and that's all.

- A wife/partner/spouse is expected to help establish a life with you, home, family, companionship, in addition to the attention and sex, and your spouse does have to do it because she is your wife and has to love you in spite of how you are.

- If men are not interested in forming a family, then perhaps patronizing prostitutes is the right solution; however, since most people ultimately do want to have a family, a long-term arrangement with a hooker probably isn't the right solution for most men.

  I am sorry the little schmuck got shredded. No one deserves that, but I don't see why "fat and ugly chicks" don't count. They're people, and as deserving of happiness as anyone else is, and it's the same for all the rest of us!

Funeral service for Mr. Underman will be at the First Christ Church at 12003 South Cincinnati, Tulsa, Oklahoma, as soon as the coroner releases the body.

Church brownies and chocolate chip cookies and half-pint cartons of whole milk will be served in the church basement. Donations in the name of Teddy will be collected for the benefit of Losers Need Love Too (LNLT).

Call for more information.

51 Let's Get a Pizza and a Beer

"Goddamn niggers," the middle-aged, bald-headed white guy sitting at the bar next to me said aloud to the television set above the bar. He was dressed in an expensive-looking suit and wearing a tie and had on what I always thought of as banker shoes—black wing tips.

I was at an upscale pub down in the French Quarter of New Orleans. I hadn't been paying attention to the news on the television above the bar, but after hearing the guy's comment, I glanced up at it. A video with people running around, police in riot gear, and burning cars was running behind the pretty woman doing the broadcast of some kind of riot. The woman's mouth was moving, but there was no sound, and from the video, I couldn't tell where the riot was taking place.

"Refill?" the bartender asked me. She was better looking than the women doing the news.

"I'd be a fool not to," I said, borrowing a line out of a novel by one of my favorite authors, Robert B. Parker.

I was not surprised the guy used the N-word. Prejudice against black people is alive and well, and not only in the United States of America but in all corners South America too—Colombia, for example.

I never worry much about it. I am an old, middle-class white guy, so I'm rarely, if ever, affected by prejudice of any kind as long as I stick in the neighborhoods where everyone looks like me, at least. I could talk about traveling outside the United States on an American passport, but that's a different story.

One of the few times prejudice intruded in my world was back in 1963, when I was a student at a small college in Tahlequah,

Oklahoma. I was on a football team with mostly white guys, but we had a couple of running backs who were black.

One was from East St. Louis and very fast. I liked him. He was always telling funny stories about growing up and how he had gotten so fast because he had to run all his life in his tough neighborhood on the east side of St. Louis to escape getting his lunch money robbed. We were not close, but he was a teammate.

"Run fast or get beat up," he told us when talking about growing up. "Same thing when playing football."

One Sunday, I got back to campus around six o'clock. There were a four of my teammates loitering around outside the athletic dorm, and the black running back from East St. Louis was one of them.

I didn't have anything to do, so I asked the guys if they wanted to go downtown to a movie at Tahlequah's theater. It was somewhat dumpy but was the only game in town. All the white guys said yes, but our black teammate shook his head no.

"My treat," I said to him, thinking he didn't have the money for the ticket.

"They won't let me in," he said.

"What are you talking about?" I said.

"They don't let black guys in at the movie theater," he told me.

"Well, fuck that," I said.

"Don't worry about it," he said. "I'm used to it."

"I'm not used to it," I said. "Let's all go get a beer and a pizza instead. I'm buying."

I might be as prejudiced as the next guy when it comes down to it, but discrimination is hard to ignore when you're dealing with it one on one. I never set foot in that movie theater again after that night.

The bartender sat my new drink on a fresh bar napkin. I picked it up, got up off my barstool, and moved to a new spot farther down the bar. I don't like bankers very much, if you want to know. I guess I am prejudiced after all.

52 All Most Old Enough

We lunched today, my daughter and I, at an old-timey kind of place down the street from our office and factory. The special today was fried chicken with a choice of five sides: mashed potatoes and gravy, corn, green beans, soup, or salad bar.

My daughter ordered the special, and rebelling against common sense, I got a deluxe hamburger with onion, lettuce and tomato, mustard, and a package of potato chips.

After we ordered and got our drinks, ice water for her and sweet iced tea for me, we got to talking about my younger brother. My daughter wanted to know why he had re-created the estate of my grandparents that he knew as a child in Decatur, Illinois, while I had not been motivated to do so. Why wasn't I rich like my brother? is what she meant.

"After all," she said, "he moved to Oklahoma when he was five years old, so most of his memories of the place came from photos and stories."

"He grew up with a nostalgic, idealized view of the place. I did not," I told her. "I remember all the good parts—the ski boat on the lake in the summers, all the family gatherings, Christmas and all the fun, everything that came with living with rich grandparents—but also how much work it was to keep the place up. My grandparents believed in hard work."

At any rate, my brother ended up with a five-acre estate worth a couple of million, and I ended up buying a house for $35,000. I live a mile from a factory that my brothers and I own. And that's just perfect, if you want to know.

He has gardeners, a pool boy, and a special place for everything. He owns luxury cars and has a beautiful blond wife whom I like very much. I have an RV that needs a new controller on the hot water heater (and has a generator that did not start the other day) and furniture that needs recovering. I could mention my life in Bogotá, Colombia; the maid that comes in five days a week; and the beautiful Colombian wife; but that would ruin the story.

I am guessing we were having the conversation about my lack of economic ambition because my daughter had recently read *Rich Dad, Poor Dad* by Robert T. Kiyosaki. I'd seen a copy of the book on her desk a couple of days ago.

Maybe she saw me as the poor dad. In my defense...well, actually, I don't have a defense. While I don't have a good excuse for not being the rich dad, I have always thought of myself as being a rich guy without the money.

"You could have been anything you wanted to be," my aunt Marsha used to say every time she saw me.

"And I *have* done so," I always replied.

Her response was to shake her head, sigh, and walk away.

"'I am educated, and that's the reason I can't do anything,'" I told my daughter, quoting some Englishman whose name I couldn't remember.

"The guy obviously was not a graduate of an English public school, where too much education would have not been an issue. You went to public school, didn't you, Dad?"

"My being educated was a joke. I should have said my seven years at university, which is not the same, taught me how to... well, not sure exactly what," I said.

"Be eternally flippant?" My daughter laughed.

"Your rich uncle picked his career early and stayed the course. Probably helped too that he chose a lucrative field in which to work. He specialized in endodontics, the dreaded root canal, steadfastly for twenty-four years. He was a piece worker all his working life."

"A piece worker?" she said.

"You know, like those women who get paid ten cents for every shirt they sew up in Bangladesh."

"Dad, he made about a thousand bucks every time he did a root canal. He did six or eight a day," she said. "You've specialized in dabbling in work mostly disguised as hobbies."

"Daddy Hinkle, your great grandfather, gave me some wonderful advice about going to work about forty years ago, and I never forgot it. 'When you are old, all you can do is work,' is what he said. 'Wait as long as you can.'"

My daughter looked at me and shook her head. She finally took a nibble out of a chicken leg.

"I took him at his word, followed his advice, and waited," I told my daughter around another big bite of burger.

"You're still waiting." She laughed.

"Well, I am trying to decide when to start up," I said after a big drink of iced tea.

"You're seventy-seven years old, Dad." She laughed.

"I am almost old enough to start working then." I laughed. "Besides, I have just finished my third book, and I like it," I said. "You want some pie for dessert?"

"Yes, I've saved room," she said.

"Okay then. Where's that waitress? I want some hot pecan pie and ice cream!"

53 Colombia

Beneath a canopy of azul
Wrapped in scent of Cattleya,
Sweat sugared forms,
One the color of espresso
Laced with hot
Honeyed milk,
Entangled in orgasmic
Stained sheets and
Afro pulsing rhythms,
Captured and intertwined,
Two foreign hearts
Melded by hungry desire,
Intoxicated by exotic heat,
Bridge two worlds
Oceans apart.

—Bogotá, 2019

About the Author

"What are you thinking about?" she asked as she stepped into a pair of open-toed high-heeled shoes and buckled the wide black belt around her small waist.

"I am trying to decide what to do with my life. Looks like I got about twenty more years left to decide. I should do it soon.

"You can email me at davidhinklesouthard@gmail.com if you want. I will respond, so think before you do," David told her.

"Email is so yesterday," she said as she opened his apartment's door and slipped outside without looking back.

www.ingramcontent.com/pod-product-compliance
Lightning Source LLC
Chambersburg PA
CBHW022058050726
47591CB00002B/590

9781954673250